7th

Social Studies

Daily Practice Workbook
20 weeks of fun activities

ARGOPREP

History

Civics and Government

Geography

Economics

ArgoPrep is one of the leading providers of supplemental educational products and services. We offer affordable and effective test prep solutions to educators, parents and students. Learning should be fun and easy! To access more resources visit us at www.argoprep.com.

Our goal is to make your life easier, so let us know how we can help you by e-mailing us at: info@argoprep.com.

- ArgoPrep is a recipient of the prestigious **Mom's Choice Award**.

- ArgoPrep also received the 2019 **Seal of Approval** from Homeschool.com for our award-winning workbooks.

- ArgoPrep was awarded the 2019 **National Parenting Products Award**, **Gold Medal Parent's Choice Award** and **the Tillywig Brain Child Award**.

ALL RIGHTS RESERVED
Copyright © 2024 by ArgoPrep
ISBN: 9781962936064

Published by Argo Brothers.

All rights reserved, no part of this book may be reproduced or distributed in any form or by any means without the written permission of Argo Brothers, Inc.

All the materials within are the exclusive property of Argo Brothers, Inc.

SOCIAL STUDIES

Social Studies Daily Practice Workbook by ArgoPrep allows students to build foundational skills and review concepts. Our workbooks explore social studies topics in depth with ArgoPrep's 5 E's to build social studies mastery.

argoprep.com

Table of Contents

Introduction

Welcome to our seventh-grade social studies workbook! This workbook has been specifically designed to help students build mastery of foundational social studies skills that are taught in seventh grade. Included are 20 weeks of comprehensive instruction covering geography as well as economic, social, and political trends.

This workbook covers eight key ideas:

NATIVE AMERICANS: The physical environment and natural resources of North America influenced the development of the first human settlements and the culture of Native Americans. Native American societies varied across North America.

COLONIAL DEVELOPMENTS: European exploration of the New World resulted in various interactions with Native Americans and in colonization. Colonial America had a variety of social structures under which not all people were treated equally.

AMERICAN INDEPENDENCE: Growing tensions over political power and economic issues sparked a movement for independence from Great Britain. New York played a critical role in the course and outcome of the American Revolution.

HISTORICAL DEVELOPMENT OF THE CONSTITUTION: The newly independent states faced political and economic struggles under the Articles of Confederation.

THE CONSTITUTION IN PRACTICE: The United States Constitution serves as the foundation of the United States government and outlines the rights of citizens. The Constitution is considered a living document that can respond to political and social changes.

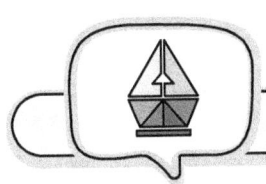

argoprep.com

WESTWARD EXPANSION: Driven by political and economic motives, the United States expanded its physical boundaries to the Pacific Ocean between 1800 and 1860. This settlement displaced Native Americans as the frontier was pushed westward.

REFORM MOVEMENTS: Social, political, and economic inequalities sparked various reform movements and resistance efforts.

A NATION DIVIDED: Westward expansion, the industrialization of the North, and the increase of slavery in the South contributed to the growth of sectionalism. Constitutional conflicts between advocates of states' rights and supporters of federal power increased tensions in the nation; attempts to compromise ultimately failed to keep the nation together, leading to the Civil War.

This workbook also includes detailed video explanations going over every page and question in the workbook. To access the video explanations, visit **argoprep.com/social7**.

How to Use the Book

All 20 weeks of daily activity pages in the book follow the same weekly structure. The activities in each of the sections align to the recommendations of the National Council for the Social Studies which help prepare students for state standardized assessments. While the sections can be completed in any order, it is important to complete each week within the section in chronological order since the skills often build upon one another.

Each week focuses on one specific topic within the section. More information about the weekly structure can be found in the Weekly Planner section.

How to access video explanations?

Go to **argoprep.com/social7**
OR scan the QR Code:

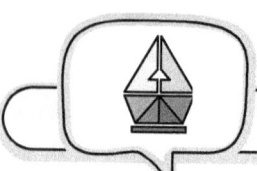
Weekly Planner

Day	Activity	Description
1	Engaging with the Topic	Read a short text on the topic and answer multiple choice questions.
2	Exploring the Topic	Interact with the topic on a deeper level by collecting, analyzing and interpreting information.
3	Explaining the Topic	Make sense of the topic by explaining and beginning to draw conclusions about information.
4	Experiencing the Topic	Investigate the topic by making real-life connections.
5	Elaborating on the Topic	Reflect on the topic and use all information learned to draw conclusions and evaluate results.

List of Topics

Unit	Week	Topic
Geography	1	America's First Peoples
Geography	2	European Exploration
History	3	Encounters and Exchanges
History	4	The British Colonies
History	5	New Netherland
Economics	6	The Growth of Slavery
History	7	Causes of the American Revolution
History	8	The War of Independence
Civics and Government	9	America Under the Articles of Confederation
Civics and Government	10	The Creation of the Constitution
Civics and Government	11	You and the Constitution
History	12	Testing the Constitution
Geography	13	Westward Expansion
Economics	14	The Early Industrialization of America
Economics	15	Slavery in America
Civics and Government	16	The Early Women's Rights Movement
Geography	17	America Divides and Compromises
History	18	The Crisis Deepens
History	19	The Civil War Begins
History	20	The War Between the States

Geography
America's First Peoples

This week, you will learn about how humans first came to the Americas. You will also learn how these people created the cultures of the Native Americans of North America.

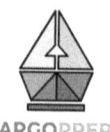
ARGOPREP

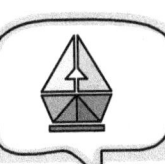
Directions: Read the text below. Then answer the questions that follow.

Scientists and archaeologists have determined that the first humans who settled in North and South America came from Asia at least 30,000 years ago. During this time, the world was in an **ice age**. Huge glaciers, some over two miles thick, covered the North and South Poles. These glaciers trapped so much water that sea levels fell, exposing land that is now underwater. Because of lower sea levels, humans had an easier time traveling between Asia and North America.

There are two major theories about how humans came to the Americas. The first is that people walked across a land bridge, called **Beringia**, between Siberia in eastern Asia and what is today Alaska. Scholars believe that people may have first crossed Beringia while following big game, such as wooly mammoths. The second theory is that people first came to the Americas by boat, spreading along the coastlines of Beringia, and migrating south along the west coast of the Americas. Those who support this theory argue that people could not have migrated by foot since large glaciers blocked access to the Americas. Archaeological evidence supports this argument.

New evidence of fossilized footprints in Mexico show that people may have come to the Americas over 40,000 years ago. These early humans were the ancestors of today's Native Americans. These people spread across the continents and evolved into a rich diversity of cultures.

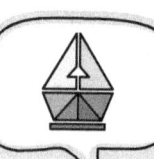
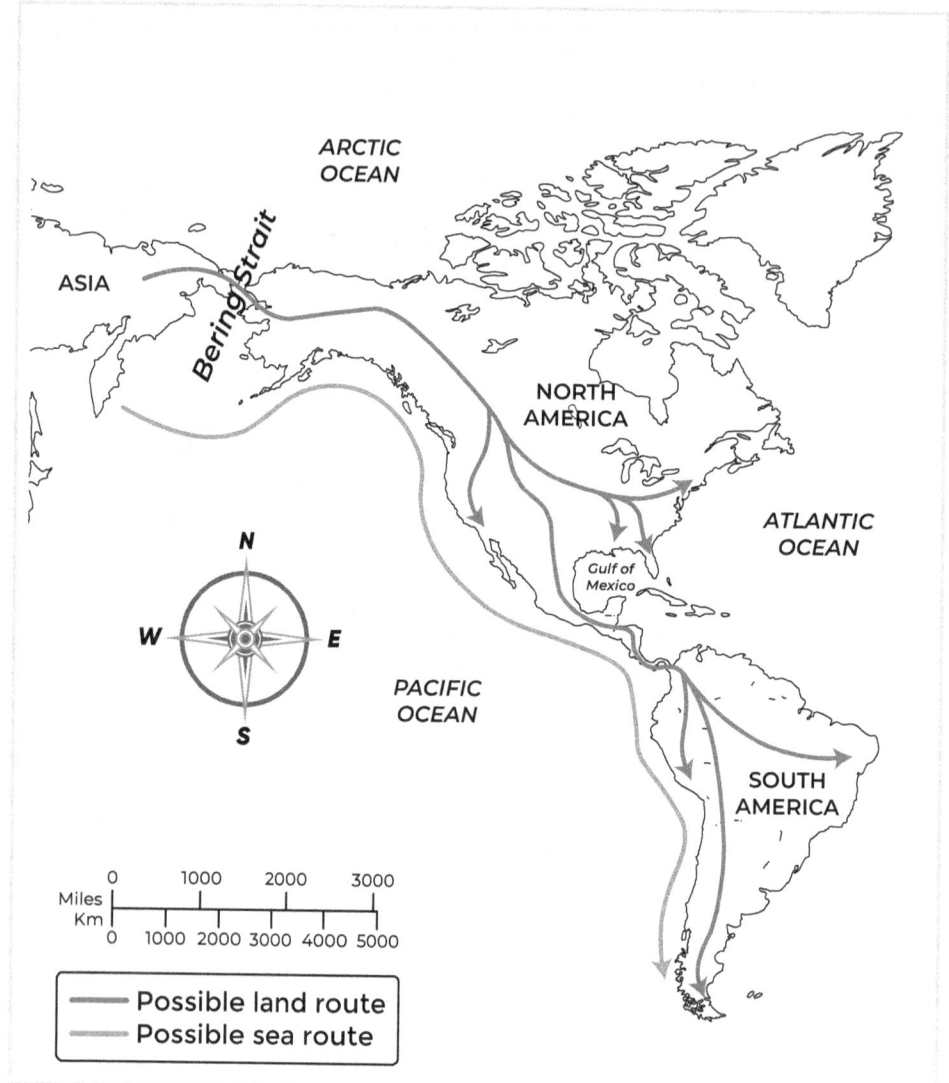

1. Most scientists and archeologists believe that the first humans of the Americas

   A. migrated from the Americas to Asia.

   B. migrated from Africa to the Americas.

   C. migrated from Europe to the Americas.

   D. migrated from Asia to the Americas.

2. What was Beringia?

   A. a land bridge that connected Asia to North America

   B. a culture of the earliest Native Americans

   C. a period of time when sea levels were lower

   D. a theory on how Native Americans arrived in the Americas

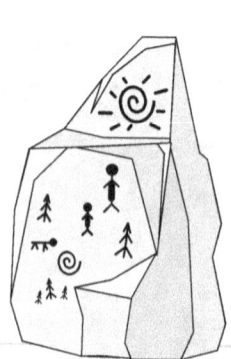

3. Scholars who support the theory that humans first arrived by boat to the Americas argue that

    A. humans could not have crossed the land due to glaciers.

    B. humans had no means of hunting large game.

    C. humans arrived in the Americas far earlier than previously thought.

    D. humans could not walk across Beringia due to high sea levels.

4. How did the Ice Age impact migration?

    A. It advanced transportation technology.

    B. It lowered sea levels allowing new ways of travel.

    C. It helped improve hunting techniques.

    D. It forced humans to migrate to new areas.

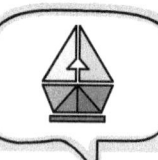
Directions: Read the text below. Then answer the questions that follow.

Yesterday you learned about how humans first migrated to the Americas. These were the ancestors of today's Native American peoples. Native Americans developed rich cultures throughout the Americas. In North America, there were hundreds of tribal groups that lived by **hunting and gathering** and by **agriculture**. Common crops included **maize**, an earlier breed of today's corn, as well as beans, squash, sunflowers, and tobacco. In the geographic area of what is now the United States and Canada, there were ten broad cultural groups.

* **Northeast** -This region features temperate forests with rivers and lakes. Many tribes practiced agriculture, as well as hunting and gathering. The Iroquois are a collection of tribes from this region.

* **Southeast** -This region is warm with fertile soil, suitable for farming. Tribes such as the Cherokee and Creek practiced large-scale agriculture and built permanent towns.

* **Plains** - This area includes the large interior region of North America containing large open prairies. Tribes in this region, such as the Comanche and Sioux, were **nomadic,** traveling from place to place to hunt animals and gather plants to eat. They were heavily influenced by the introduction of horses to North America by the Spanish, which helped them travel across greater distances.

* **Great Basin** - This is a desert region where tribes such as the Ute lived subsistence lifestyles, getting everything they needed to survive from the plants and animals around them. They, like the Plains tribes, were heavily influenced by the introduction of the horse.

* **Plateau** - This region features rivers and streams where tribes such as the Nez Perce survived through fishing and gathering. The tribes in the Plateau region were mostly nomadic.

* **Southwest** - This arid region was home to farming people such as the Hopi and Zuni, as well as nomadic people like the Apache who were hunter-gatherers. Tribes in the Southwest region lived in mud homes or carved homes into cliffs.

* **California** - This region, which is roughly in the area of modern California, had a temperate climate and was home to about 100 different tribes of hunter-gatherers, such as the Mojave and Paiute. Some of these tribes also practiced small-scale agriculture.

* **Northwest Coast** - This region, with a mild, wet climate, had plentiful natural resources such as salmon, sea otters, and many edible plants and berries to gather and grow. Tribes in this region, such as the Haida, were able to establish permanent villages due to the abundance of resources.

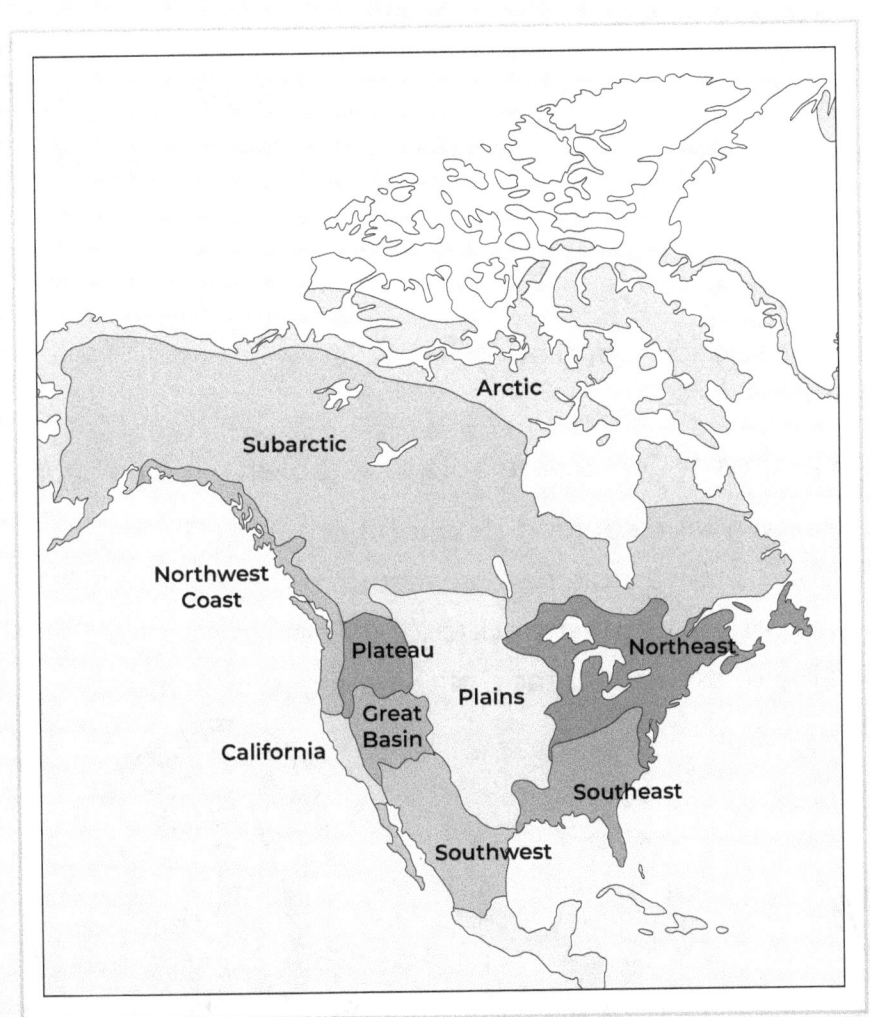

Native American cultural regions in North America

* **Subarctic** - This region stretches across much of Canada through inland Alaska. Native American tribes, such as the Ojibwa, survived through hunting, fishing, and gathering in small groups.

* **Arctic** - This inhospitable region in the north has long periods of darkness and cold weather. Tribes such as the Aleut and Inuit, survived by hunting and fishing.

1. How did the introduction of horses impact Plains cultures?

A. They were able to use the horses for farming.

B. They were able to build permanent settlements.

C. They were able to gather more plants.

D. They were able to travel across greater distances.

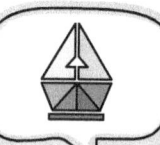
2. Why was the Arctic region less densely populated with people than other regions?

    A. because of its thick forests   **C.** because of its extremely cold climate

    B. because of its overly wet climate   **D.** because of its lack of water

3. What is a shared feature of the Northeast and Southeast Native American cultural groups?

    A. They both lived in inhospitable regions.

    B. They both had agriculture.

    C. They both featured low population levels.

    D. They both were nomadic.

4. Tribes on the Northwest Coast were able to establish villages because

    A. They had an abundance of food through farming.

    B. They were able to use ample natural resources.

    C. They took advantage of the introduction of horses.

    D. They were able to take advantage of the arid environment.

Directions: Read the text below. Then answer the questions that follow.

You have learned about the different cultural groups of Native Americans and how geography impacted their lifestyles. Today you will learn about how the geography of what is now New York State impacted the development of various Northeast tribes. As you learned yesterday, this region features a diverse geography of rivers, mountains, lakes, and forests. As a result, Native American tribes in what is now New York State were able to develop agriculture, as well as take advantage of the region's natural resources by hunting, fishing, and gathering.

There were many tribes in what is now New York State. The **Iroquois Confederacy**, also known as the **Haudenosaunee**, was a collection of tribes who shared a central government. These tribes included the Seneca, Mohawk, Onondaga, Oneida, Cayuga, and, much later, the Tuscarora. The Iroquois Confederacy was formed in the 1100s by **Hiawatha**, who went on to become their first leader. The structure of the Iroquois Confederacy would later influence the development of the United States government by showing a framework for how different states could unite.

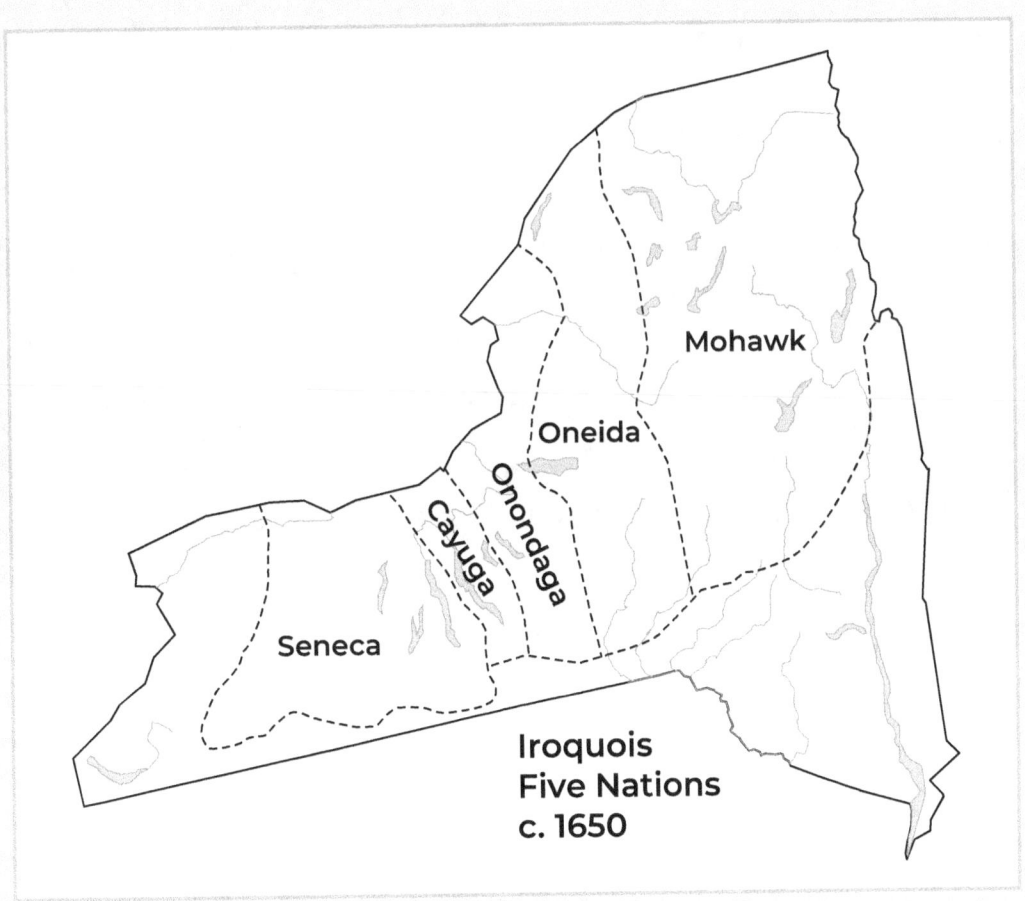

Mohawk

Oneida

Onondaga

Cayuga

Seneca

Iroquois
Five Nations
c. 1650

"

The tribes of the Iroquois confederacy lived in small villages made of multiple **longhouses**. These were buildings made of saplings, or young trees, and covered with bark. Men fished and hunted and took part in war while women gathered wild food and tended to crops such as squash, beans, and maize. Warfare was an important aspect of Iroquois life, with frequent raids resulting in the capturing and enslavement of people from neighboring tribes, such as the Lenni Lenape, often to replace those killed in conflict.

"

1. A central feature of Iroquois villages were

   A. farms

   B. forts

   C. longhouses

   D. markets

2. What role did women have in Iroquois life?

   A. farming and gathering

   B. hunting

   C. warfare

   D. fishing

3. What was the Iroquois Confederacy?

   ....

   ....

   ....

4. How did the Iroquois Confederacy influence the structure of the United States government?

   ....

   ....

   ....

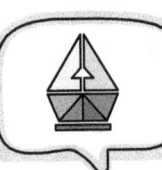
Directions: Read the text below. Then answer the questions that follow.

Native American cultures have impacted the different regions of North America in unique ways. Consider where you live and then research and respond to the following questions.

1. What Native American tribes lived where you now reside?

_____

_____

_____

_____

_____

2. What are some examples of Native American place names close to you?

_____

_____

_____

_____

_____

3. How many Native American tribes exist in New York today? Which one is closest to you?

_____

_____

_____

_____

_____

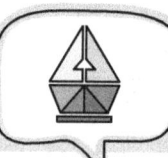
Directions: Read the text below. Then answer the questions that follow.

This week you learned about the migration of humans into the Americas and the establishment of Native American cultures. You also learned about the Iroquois of New York State.

1. How does geography play a role in the development of cultural groups?

2. How does geography help determine the population density of a given area?

3. How did geography help develop the society of the Iroquois?

4. Complete the following chart by filling in the geographic features of the identified Native American cultural regions with the terms below the chart.

Region	Geographic features
Northeast	
Plains	
Southwest	
Pacific Northwest	
Arctic	

Features to fill in: Rich natural resources, Long winters, Woodlands, Prairie, Arid

Geography
European Exploration

This week, you will learn about how Europeans in the 1400s began to explore the world and expand European influence in North and South America.

ARGOPREP

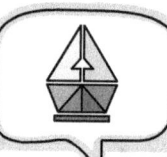
Directions: Read the text below. Then answer the questions that follow.

Last week, you learned about the first humans to settle in the Americas and the origins of Native American cultures. These cultures were greatly impacted by the arrival of Europeans in the late 1400s. Over the course of centuries, Europeans displaced Native American peoples often through the use of force or the impact of disease.

Europeans were first motivated to come to the Americas for economic reasons. Until the 1400s, people in Europe had only heard stories of what lay beyond the vast Atlantic Ocean. Stories of travelers, such as Lief Erikson, told of distant lands. In the 1200s, Europeans had begun to have more contact through trade with countries in Asia. From Asia, Europeans acquired valuable luxury items such as spices and silk, which were in great demand. The problem was that these goods passed through the hands of so many people to reach Europe that their prices were very high. Countries in the west of Europe such as Portugal and Spain wanted to find new routes directly to Asia in order to decrease the cost of those goods. They were hoping to find a route to Asia directly by sea.

Europe benefited from new inventions that enhanced the ability of ships to voyage by sea. Through the study of Arabic texts, Europeans learned about the **astrolabe**, which was a tool used to help determine a ship's position at sea. Another valuable tool was the **magnetic compass**, which allowed navigators to know which direction was North. In addition, Portugal developed a new kind of ship called the **caravel**, which incorporated new ship technology. The caravel used a new combination of sails including triangular **lateen sails** which allowed it to sail against the wind. It also had a more effective placement of the ship's rudder. The caravel was able to successfully sail over deep water. It was on caravels that the Portuguese explorer, Bartolomeu Dias, reached the southern tip of Africa in 1488 while trying to find a way to Asia.

It was in this context that would-be explorers began to rediscover old geography texts. One of these explorers was an Italian navigator named Christopher Columbus who proposed that a ship sailing west across the Atlantic could reach Asia. After his ideas were rejected by other countries, such as Portugal, he convinced Queen Isabella and King Ferdinand of Spain to sponsor a voyage west. He set sail with three ships in August 1492.

A caravel

1. What was an astrolabe used for?

A. navigation   **B.** trade   **C.** speed   **D.** warfare

2. Which country sponsored Columbus's voyage?

A. England   **B.** Portugal   **C.** France   **D.** Spain

3. Europeans in Western Europe originally wanted to find a sea route to Asia in order to

A. set up new colonies.

B. enhance scientific knowledge of sailing.

C. profit from the trade of luxury goods.

D. rediscover ancient learning.

4. The passing of luxury goods, such as silk and spices, from Asia to Europe through many different hands resulted in

A. new technology.   **C.** lower demand.

B. high prices.   **D.** decreased trade.

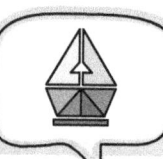
Directions: Read the text below. Then answer the questions that follow.

Christopher Columbus landed on an island, now the Bahamas, in the Caribbean Sea on October 12, 1492. Columbus believed that he had reached the Indies, the islands in East Asia that possessed valuable spices. Therefore, when he wrote about the Native Americans, he referred to them as Indians.

After Columbus returned to Spain, other European explorers began making the journey to the Americas. These men explored North and South America and established claims for their country's control of these areas, regardless of the presence of Native Americans. In Central America, a group of **conquistadors**, or Spanish conquerors, under the command of Hernán Cortés, conquered the Aztec empire through warfare and disease. The table below shows more explorers from the European Age of Exploration.

Explorer	Country He Explored For	Area Explored
John Cabot	England	An Italian explorer whose real name was Giovanni Caboto, he explored the northeastern coast of North America in the 1490s. He established claims for England in North America.
Jacques Cartier	France	He explored and mapped the area of the St. Lawrence River in three voyages starting in 1534. He established claims for France in today's Canada.

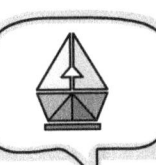
Explorer	Country He Explored For	Area Explored
Samuel de Champlain	France	He founded the city of Quebec and the colony of New France in 1608. He also explored areas of the Great Lakes.
Vasco da Gama	Portugal	His voyage from 1497 to 1499 was the first in which Europeans sailed around Africa to Asia. He allowed Portugal to have a powerful role in East Asia.
Henry Hudson	The Netherlands/ England	He sailed for the Netherlands and England searching for a northwest passage from North America to Asia. He explored today's New York and voyaged up the river bearing his name. He disappeared in 1611 after his crew mutinied and abandoned him. He claimed areas in today's New York for the Netherlands and areas of Canada for England.

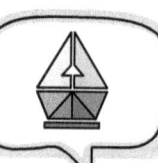
Explorer	Country He Explored For	Area Explored
Ferdinand Magellan	Spain	His expedition was the first to circumnavigate the globe (1519 - 1522) although Magellan himself died during the voyage.
Giovanni da Verrazzano	France	He explored the East Coast of North America in 1524 and provided information on the size of the continent.

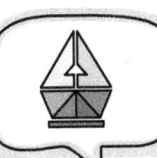
1. Who established claims for the Netherlands in the region of today's New York?

    A. John Cabot

    B. Henry Hudson

    C. Vasco da Gama

    D. Ferdinand Magellan

2. Who were the conquistadors?

    A. English explorers who journeyed to North America

    B. Spanish conquerors who took over Central American empires

    C. French navigators looking for a Northwest Passage

    D. Portuguese sailors seeking a sea route around Africa

3. New France was established by

    A. Giovanni da Verrazzano

    B. Jacques Cartier

    C. Ferdinand Magellan

    D. Samuel de Champlain

4. _____ sailing for Portugal found a sea route around Africa to Asia.

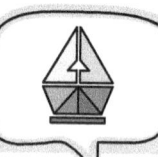
Directions: Read the text below. Then answer the questions that follow.

Maps are helpful tools which can be used to illustrate historic events. The map below shows the different routes European explorers took while seeking a sea route to Asia.

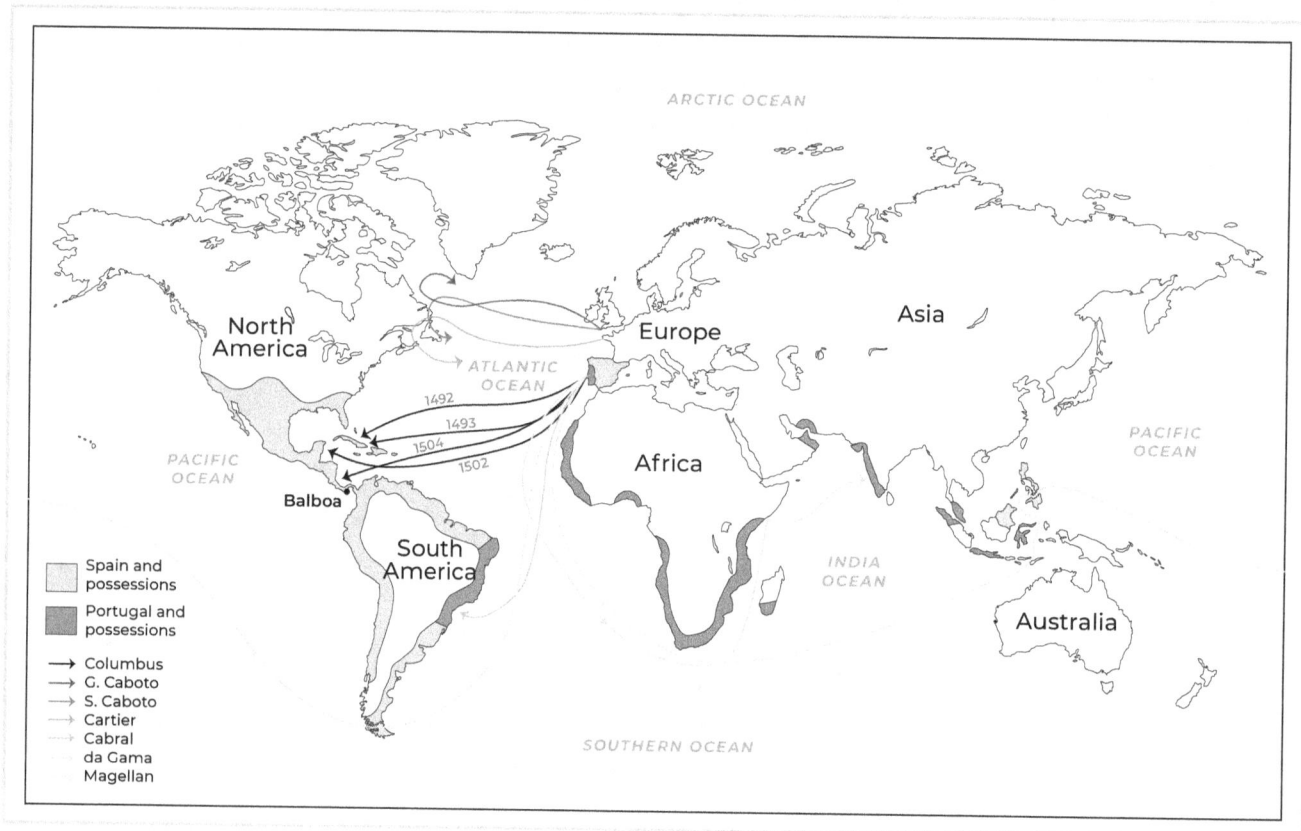

1. Based on the map, how many all water routes to Asia from Europe did explorers find? ....

2. Based on the map, how many times did Columbus travel to the Americas?
....

3. Which water route from Europe to Asia seems to be the easiest route?
....

4. On this map, where were most of Portugal's possessions? ....

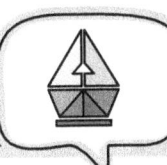
Directions: Read the text below. Then answer the questions that follow.

This excerpt is from the journal of Christopher Columbus dated December 16, 1492:

For I, with the force I have under me, which is not large, could march over all these islands without opposition. I have seen only three sailors land, without wishing to do harm, and a multitude of Indians fled before them. They have no arms, and are without warlike instincts; they all go naked, and are so timid that a thousand would not stand before three of our men. So that they are good to be ordered about, to work and sow, and do all that may be necessary, and to build towns, and they should be taught to go about clothed and to adopt our customs.

1. What attitude does Columbus have toward Native Americans?

_____

_____

_____

2. What does Columbus imply should happen to Native Americans?

_____

_____

_____

_____

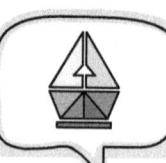
Directions: Read the text below. Then answer the questions that follow.

This week you learned about the exploration of the world by Europeans and how it established a European presence in the Americas.

1. How did economic need drive discovery during the Age of Exploration?

_____

_____

_____

_____

_____

2. How did the attitudes of Columbus and other explorers and conquistadors towards Native Americans impact their actions? Support your answer with an example from the readings.

_____

_____

_____

_____

_____

3. Do you think the conquest of the Aztec Empire by the Spanish was inevitable? Why or why not?

_____

_____

_____

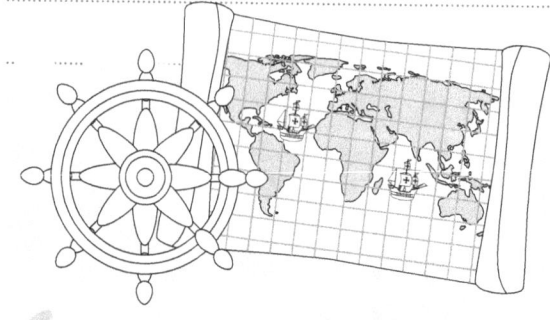

_____

_____

CONQUISTADOR

History

Encounters and Exchanges

WEEK 3

ARGOPREP

This week, you will learn about the Columbian Exchange and its impact on Native Americans.

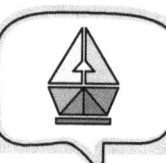

Directions: Read the text below. Then answer the questions that follow.

Last week, you learned about European exploration and how the countries of Spain, France, England, and the Netherlands claimed lands in North and South America. The act of taking over lands and creating settlements is called **colonization**. The creation of European **colonies** in the Americas led to increased encounters and exchanges with Native Americans. Plants, animals, and even ideas and diseases were traded between the Americas and Europe. Historians refer to this as the **Columbian Exchange**. Foods such as tomatoes, peppers, and potatoes were taken from the Americas and brought to Europe. Europeans introduced livestock such as horses to the Americas, which had a major impact on the Native American tribes of the Great Plains. Europeans also brought diseases with them from Europe to the Americas. Infections such as smallpox, measles, and cholera, which had long been present in Europe, ran rampant among Native Americans, who had no natural immunity to the diseases. Historians estimate that disease killed over 90% of the Native American population. Read through the chart below to learn more about the Columbian Exchange.

	From Europe to the Americas	**From Americas to Europe**
Animals	Horse, donkey, sheep, pig, cow, chickens, cat, goat	Alpaca, turkey, llama
Disease	Small pox, measles, influenza, mumps, malaria, yellow fever	Syphilis
Plants	Rice, wheat, bananas, oranges, coffee, sugar, barley, grapes, lemons, watermelon	Potato, maize (corn), tomato, tobacco, peppers, peanuts, pumpkins, sweet potatoes

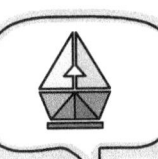
1. Which of the following is an example of a plant that was brought from Europe to the Americas?

   A. potato

   B. pumpkin

   C. tomato

   D. barley

2. Why were European diseases so deadly to Native Americans?

   A. Native Americans did not have immunity to European diseases.

   B. Native Americans did not have the technology to fight diseases.

   C. Native Americans did not have natural resources to fight diseases.

   D. Native Americans did not have medicine to fight diseases.

3. Which of the following is an example of an animal that was brought from the Americas to Europe?

   A. chicken

   B. turkey

   C. horse

   D. goat

4. What would be a direct benefit of the Columbian Exchange?

   A. more diverse food sources

   B. more arable land

   C. improved technology

   D. improved relations among people

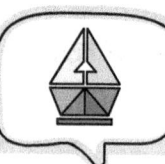
Directions: Read the text below. Then answer the questions that follow.

By the 1500s, Spain had effectively colonized most of the Caribbean, South America, and Central America. Much of this was done through the efforts of the conquistadors who extended Spanish rule. The motives of the conquistadors were gold, glory, and God. That is, they were interested in finding riches, bringing fame to themselves, and spreading their Christian faith. The most successful of the conquistadors were Hernán Cortés and Francisco Pizarro. Cortés conquered the Aztec Empire, and Francisco Pizarro ruthlessly conquered the Incan Empire in Peru. Both conquests brought immense wealth to the Spanish Empire and inspired other conquistadors.

Some conquistadors explored areas of North America that would later become part of the United States. One of these was Juan Ponce de León who explored modern day Florida in 1513 and again in 1521. Leon was searching for an island which was rumored to have a "fountain of youth" that rejuvenated those who drank from it. During his 1521 expedition he came into conflict with Native Americans and was killed.

Another conquistador was Hernando de Soto. As a young man, he accompanied conquistadors to Peru and helped conquer the Incan Empire, bringing much wealth to Spain. De Soto wanted to follow in the footsteps of his predecessors. He launched an expedition of 700 men through Florida and crossed over the mainland United States, fighting Native Americans along the way and killing hundreds. His was the first European expedition to find the immense Mississippi River in 1541. The next year, while still on the expedition, de Soto died from illness.

A third conquistador was Francisco Vázquez de Coronado. He was the governor of New Spain (today's Mexico) who heard rumors about seven cities of gold to the north. He launched an expedition in 1540 into the southwestern part of the United States. He, like the other conquistadors, engaged in violent conflicts along the way, this time with the Zuni tribe. Coronado never found any cities of gold and returned to New Spain in 1542.

CONQUISTADOR

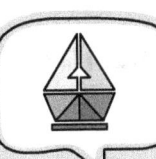
1. Who was the conquistador who explored Florida?

   A. Francisco Vázquez de Coronado.

   B. Juan Ponce de León

   C. Hernando de Soto

   D. Francisco Pizarro

2. The conquistador _____ was an inspiration to other conquistadors because of his conquest of the Aztec Empire.

   A. Hernán Cortés

   B. Francisco Pizarro

   C. Juan Ponce de León

   D. Francisco Vázquez de Coronado.

3. How might Native Americans have viewed the conquistadors?

   ....

   ....

   ....

4. What were some of the long-term effects and consequences of the conquistadors' actions?

   ....

   ....

   ....

Directions: Read the text below. Then answer the questions that follow.

The Columbian Exchange resulted in the deaths of 90% of the Native American population. Exactly how many people lived in the Americas before Columbus is unknown. Some historians believe that around 900,000 Native Americans lived in what is now the United States and Canada before Columbus invaded, while others estimate a population as high as 18 million.

The Columbian exchange also resulted in changes to Native American cultures. The most dramatic example of this was the adoption of horses by the Native American tribes of the Great Plains. Horses originally evolved in North America, but went extinct between 8 to 12 thousand years ago after spreading to Asia. Native Americans on the Great Plains were hunter-gatherers that relied on foot power and the use of dogs as pack animals.

The conquistadors brought horses with them to Central America in the 1500s. Many horses escaped. Herds of wild horses roamed north to the Great Plains. The plains tribes began domesticating these wild horses and using them to hunt large herds of bison. Previously hunting bison on foot, the use of horses revolutionized people's ability to travel across greater distances and hunt more game. By the 19th century, when tribes such as the Apaches, Dakota, and Cheyenne began to come into contact with American settlers moving west, they had already been taming horses for centuries. These tribes were considered some of the greatest horse-riding cultures in history. Their use of horses in warfare also helped them resist many invasions of their lands by American armies.

1. How did the use of horses impact Native Americans on the Great Plains?

   A. It resulted in an expansion of Spanish power.

   B. It helped them travel greater distances and hunt more successfully.

   C. It forced them to adopt more permanent lifestyles in villages.

   D. It enhanced agriculture by encouraging them to plant new foods.

2. What was something that horses allowed Native American tribes to hunt more effectively?

   A. goats   **B.** bison   **C.** turkeys   **D.** rabbits

3. Was the Columbian Exchange more beneficial or harmful? Explain your reasoning.

Directions: Read the text below. Then answer the questions that follow.

Álvar Núñez Cabeza de Vaca was a Spanish conquistador in an expedition led by Pánfilo de Narváez. In 1527, they traveled to Tampa Bay with the intent of conquering the land for Spain. The expedition met disaster, however, when Cabeza de Vaca found himself shipwrecked and then enslaved by a local tribe in 1529. The would-be conqueror learned the customs of his captors and later became a trader, interacting with various tribes all along the Gulf Coast and into the American Southwest. In 1536, he came to the outskirts of New Spain where he encountered Spaniards enslaving Native Americans. A survivor of slavery himself, he was disgusted by the treatment of Native Americans at the hands of the Spanish. He later wrote an account of his journeys, which became one of the earliest detailed accounts of Native American culture and customs.

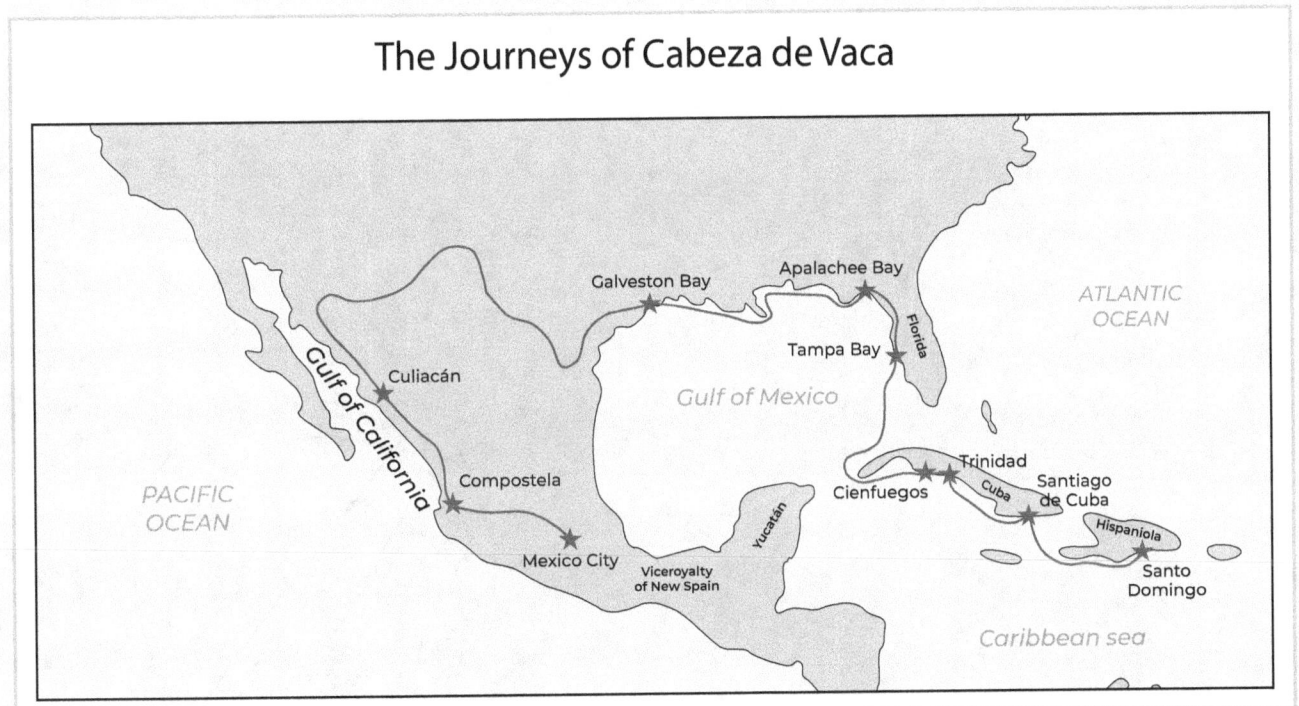

The Journeys of Cabeza de Vaca

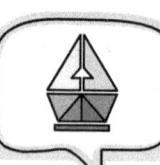
1. Explain how the experiences of Cabeza de Vaca transformed him.

....

....

....

....

....

....

2. Why are the experiences of Cabeza de Vaca relevant today?

....

....

....

....

....

....

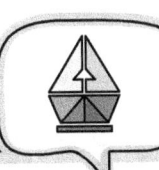
Directions: Read the text below. Then answer the questions that follow.

This week you learned about the Columbian Exchange and its impact.

1. Who benefited the most from the Columbian Exchange? Explain your thinking.

....

....

....

....

2. How might religion have been used at the time to justify colonization?

....

....

....

....

3. Why is the Columbian Exchange relevant today?

....

....

....

....

....

WEEK 4

History

The British Colonies

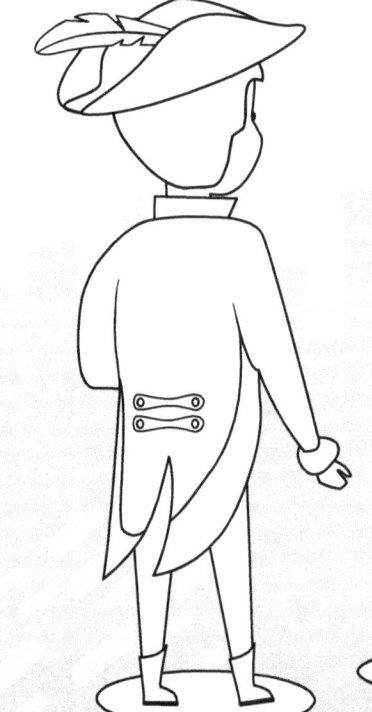

This week, you will learn about the establishment of the thirteen British colonies in America and the differences between the different colonies.

ARGOPREP

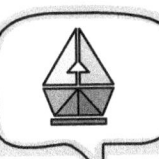
Directions: Read the text below. Then answer the questions that follow.

By the 1500s, Spain controlled most of the Caribbean, South America, and Central America. Other countries who were rivals of Spain wanted to establish colonies of their own. Nations like England, France, and the Netherlands turned their attention to North America, where Spain was largely inactive. The exception to this would be the city of St. Augustine, Florida, founded by Spain in 1565, making it the oldest city in the United States today.

The first successful non-Spanish colony in North America was founded by France in 1608 with the establishment of Quebec and the colony of New France, which is now in Canada. The next year, the Netherlands established New Amsterdam in what is now New York City. Both the French and Dutch colonies were centered on the fur trade, and never had large numbers of permanent colonists.

The first two British colonies in North America were established in Jamestown, Virginia, in 1607, and in Plymouth, Massachusetts, in 1620. Jamestown was founded by a **joint-stock company** called the Virginia Company. A joint stock company is a group of people who invest money to make a profit. This company invested in the colony of Jamestown in order to make money off of the goods that could be shipped back to Europe from the Americas. Plymouth was established by people who became known as the **pilgrims**. A number of these pilgrims were religious dissenters called **Separatists** who had moved from England to the Netherlands to escape persecution, before founding their own religious colony in North America.

Both Jamestown and Plymouth struggled in their early years. The first years were marked by extensive starvation, which almost made both colonies collapse. Jamestown survived due to the support of the local Native American tribes and also because the colony began to make money through the growth of tobacco. The pilgrims in Plymouth also survived with the help of local tribes and in a few years became self-sufficient.

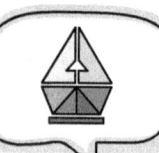

1. Why were the British and French interested in establishing colonies in North America?
   A. because of the rich civilizations that could be conquered
   B. because its climate made it easier to settle
   C. because Spain was occupying other areas in the Americas
   D. because the land was uninhabited

2. What was the motive behind the foundation of the Jamestown colony?
   A. politics
   B. glory
   C. religion
   D. profit

3. Who founded what became modern-day New York?
   A. Britain
   B. France
   C. Spain
   D. the Netherlands

4. Who were the Separatists?
   A. religious dissenters who left England
   B. fur traders from New France
   C. merchants from the Netherlands
   D. settlers who traveled to Jamestown

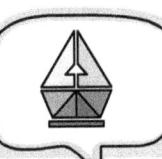
Directions: Read the text below. Then answer the questions that follow.

By the mid-18th century, Britain had established thirteen separate colonies along the east coast of North America. These colonies, unlike those of Spain, were decentralized, each having their own local governments, though they were still under the control of Britain. There were three major geographic areas for the British colonies: New England, the Middle Colonies, and the Southern Colonies.

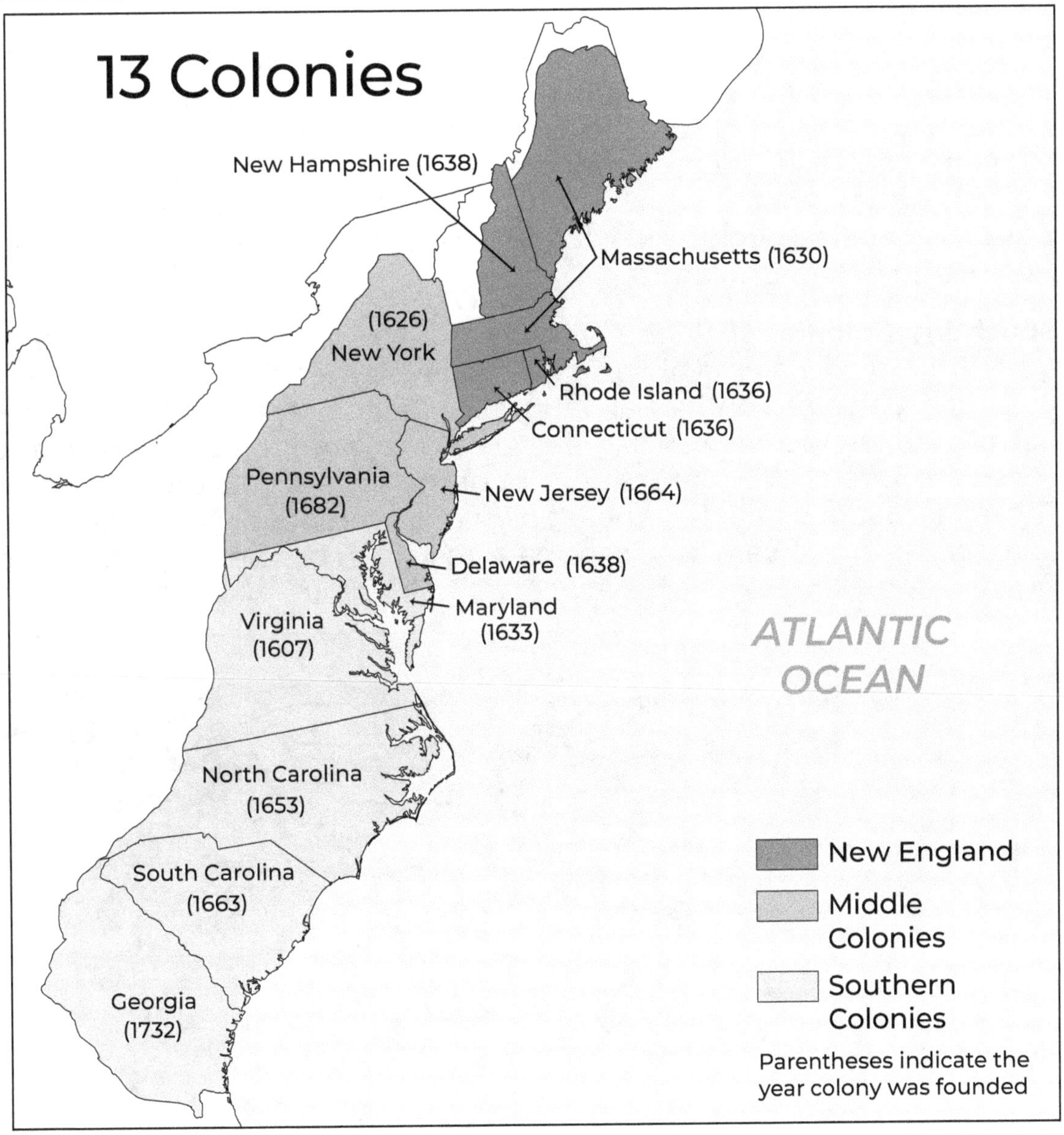

13 Colonies

New Hampshire (1638)

Massachusetts (1630)

(1626)
New York

Rhode Island (1636)

Connecticut (1636)

Pennsylvania (1682)

New Jersey (1664)

Delaware (1638)

Maryland (1633)

Virginia (1607)

ATLANTIC OCEAN

North Carolina (1653)

South Carolina (1663)

Georgia (1732)

New England

Middle Colonies

Southern Colonies

Parentheses indicate the year colony was founded

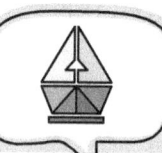
The **New England** colonies included Massachusetts, Connecticut, Rhode Island, and New Hampshire. Their largest city was Boston. These colonies were mostly founded by different Christian religious groups that wanted to establish their own societies that followed rules based on their religion. Many of the colonists in New England were **Puritans**, members of a religious reform movement who were intolerant of other religions. As a result, New England colonies consisted of many small, self-sufficient villages and communities. New England did not have the best climate or soil for agriculture. Instead, due to the numerous **bays** along the coast, colonists relied on fishing and whaling as a way to make money.

The **Middle Colonies** included New York, New Jersey, Delaware, and Pennsylvania. These colonies were generally more tolerant of different religions than the New England colonies, and had more diverse settlers from different countries in Europe. The Middle Colonies had a more mild climate than New England and more fertile soil. As a result, there were more farms than in New England. With enough crops to feed many people, this region saw the growth of several large cities, including Philadelphia and New York, which developed on large rivers like the Hudson and Delaware. In the cities, people worked in shops to manufacture different products that were sent back to England.

The **Southern Colonies** included Virginia, North Carolina, South Carolina, and Georgia. The region was mainly rural with a few larger cities, such as Charleston, South Carolina. This region had a warm climate and fertile soils. As a result, the Southern Colonies focused on large-scale agriculture. Large-scale **plantations** grew **cash crops**, or crops that made a lot of money, such as tobacco, indigo, and rice. These plantations relied on the labor of enslaved people to plant and harvest these crops. The crops were then sent back to Britain or sold to the other colonies.

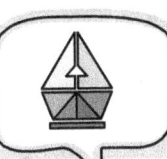
1. The Southern Colonies had an economy based on

A. industry

B. agriculture

C. fishing

D. trade

2. Which of the following colonies was a part of New England?

A. Virginia

B. Delaware

C. North Carolina

D. Connecticut

3. New England was marked by

A. religious tolerance

B. warm climate

C. rich soil

D. numerous bays

4. A large city in the Middle Colonies was

A. New York

B. Boston

C. Charleston

D. Jamestown

Directions: Read the text below. Then answer the questions that follow.

The British colonies developed in different ways. All colonies were allowed to exist under a **charter** from the British Crown, which was a contract that made the colony legal. However, the details of each of these charters were different. A colony could be a royal colony, proprietary colony, or charter colony. A **royal colony**, also known as a **provincial colony** meant it was ruled under the British Crown, with its governors being selected by the British government. One example is New York, which became a royal colony in 1664 when the English took control of New Netherland. A **proprietary colony** existed under a charter that allowed a single person, the **proprietor**, to run the colony under the British government. An example of this would be Maryland, which was set up as a proprietary colony under Lord Baltimore in 1633 as a haven for English Catholics. Another example is Pennsylvania, which was a proprietary colony under William Penn and was founded in 1682 for the religious sect known as the Quakers. A **charter colony**, sometimes called a joint-stock colony, was a colony run by investors in the hopes of making a profit. Colonies could change from one type of charter to another. For example, Virginia and Massachusetts started as joint-stock colonies but later became royal colonies.

Each of the colonies also developed their own form of self-government. Virginia, for example, established the **House of Burgesses** in 1619, which was the first **legislature**, or law-making body, in colonial America. In other regions, such as New England, colonies had a greater focus on local communities and instead made decisions through **town meetings** where the citizens of a community would directly discuss and decide upon issues. As for Britain, it generally allowed the colonies to run their own affairs in a policy called **salutary neglect**. This allowed ideas of self-government and independence from Britain to take root.

1. A colony where the British government directly appointed the colonial governors is a

    A. proprietary colony

    B. charter colony

    C. provincial colony

    D. joint-stock colony

2. How did Britain's policy of salutary neglect help develop democracy in the colonies?

    A. It allowed the different colonial sections to grow economically.

    B. It allowed the colonies to get used to self-government.

    C. It allowed the crown to appoint officials to run the colonies.

    D. It created a contract for the colonies, making it legal.

3. Which of the following colonies was founded as proprietary colony meant to protect English Catholics?

    A. Maryland

    B. Pennsylvania

    C. New York

    D. Massachusetts

4. Why was the House of Burgesses important?

....

....

....

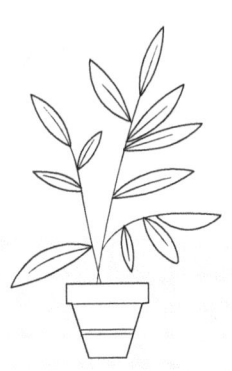

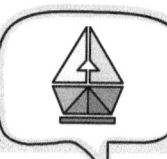
Directions: Read the text below. Then answer the questions that follow.

As you have learned, geography played an important role in shaping the American colonies. Consider the geography of your own community — for example, the shape of the land, nearness to waterways, or access to natural resources.

1. Describe some of the geographic features of your community.

_____

_____

_____

_____

_____

2. How has geography helped shape your community?

_____

_____

_____

_____

_____

_____

Directions: Read the text below. Then answer the questions that follow.

This week you learned about the thirteen British colonies in North America. You also learned how these colonies developed differently based on their geographic characteristics and forms of government.

1. If you were a colonist, would you prefer to live in a charter, proprietary, or royal colony? Explain your reasoning.

2. Throughout their history, there was a trend for proprietary and charter colonies to become royal colonies at the request of the colonists. What may have been a reason for this?

3. How may policies such as salutary neglect have pushed the colonies toward independence?

History

New Netherland

This week, you will learn about the Dutch colony of New Netherland that would become today's New York.

ARGOPREP

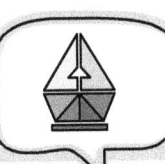
Directions: Read the text below. Then answer the questions that follow.

New York was unique among the thirteen colonies since it was not founded by British colonists. Instead, it was founded by the Dutch in 1614 under the West India Company of the Netherlands. The Netherlands claimed the region based on the explorations of Henry Hudson in 1609. They hired Hudson to seek a northern all-water route to Asia. In 1624, the Netherlands sent its first group of permanent colonists, under Director General Peter Minuit, to settle at the mouth of the North River, which is now called the Hudson River. There, they established New Amsterdam on today's Manhattan Island after purchasing the island from the Lenape people. The Dutch established other trading posts along the Hudson River up to Fort Orange which is now Albany. The Dutch traded manufactured goods with Native American tribes such as the Iroquois and Mahican in exchange for furs such as beaver pelts. New Netherland grew to include most of New Jersey and portions of Connecticut, although these areas did not have many Dutch colonists, and were still inhabited by native peoples. The Dutch wanted these lands because of their interest in expanding the fur trade.

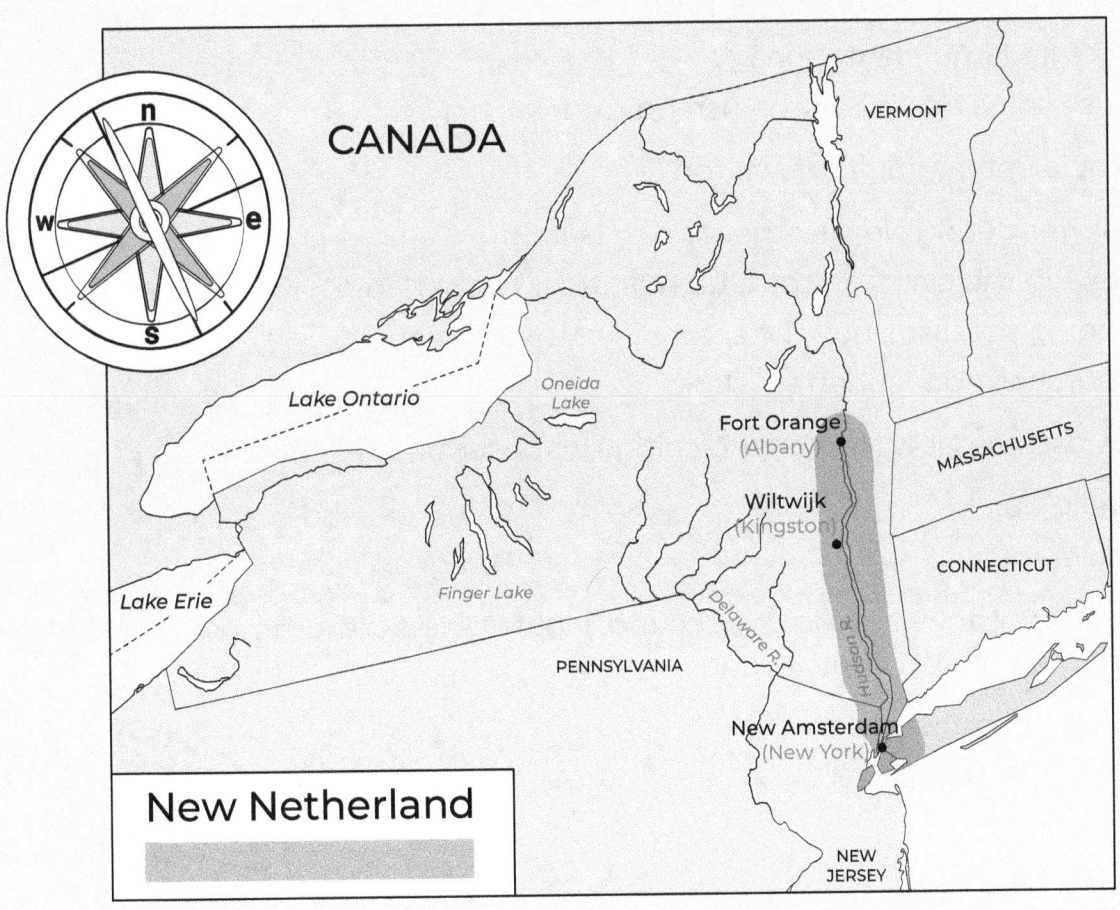

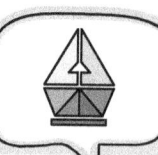
"

In New Amsterdam, a diverse colony developed. By 1645, there were no more than 500 people living in New Amsterdam, but they spoke about 18 different languages, and a large portion of the population was not Dutch. The colony was tolerant of many religions and people. New Netherland also gave more rights to women than other European colonies. Despite its diversity, the Dutch colony saw slow population growth in its early years. In the end, it flourished under its last director, Peter Stuyvesant. The neighboring colonies in New England greatly outnumbered the Dutch. The colony was captured by the English in 1664 and renamed New York, after the Duke of York. However, Dutch culture and influence would remain strong in New York and would influence American culture and political traditions.

"

1. New Netherland was primarily founded to

   A. provide a safe haven for religious dissenters.

   B. take advantage of the fur trade.

   C. create large plantations.

   D. use ships to expand the fishing trade.

2. What is Peter Minuit known for?

   A. surrendering New Netherland to Britain

   B. laying the claim for the Dutch on New Netherland

   C. being the last Dutch Director of New Netherland

   D. purchasing Manhattan Island

3. How can the New Netherland colony be described?

   A. religious

   B. tolerant

   C. militaristic

   D. agricultural

4. According to the map in this section, what is the northernmost settlement in New Netherland?

   A. Fort Orange

   B. New Amsterdam

   C. Wiltwijk

   D. Kingston

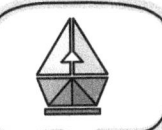
Directions: Read the text below. Then answer the questions that follow.

New Netherland was a small colony compared to the neighboring colonies in New England to the east. However, by the 1650s, the colony had become important because of the natural advantages of the harbor of New Amsterdam. It also fostered strategic alliances between the Dutch and the Native Americans, specifically the Iroquois. The Dutch were different from other European colonists since they did not actively seek to convert Native Americans to Christianity. This is not to say that New Netherland did not come into conflict with Native Americans like other Europeans. From 1643 to 1645, the Dutch Director-General Willem Kieft went to war with the Lenape after they refused to pay tribute. This war, called Kieft's War, resulted in Native Americans in the region uniting against the Dutch and disrupting trade in the region. Many colonists returned to the Netherlands. After colonists complained about Kieft and his policies against Native Americans, he was recalled.

Peter Stuyvesant

Kieft's successor was Peter Stuyvesant who was the most famous of New Netherlands Director-Generals. He was a devoted officer of the Dutch West India Company and had even lost a leg in the Caribbean during a battle. Stuyvesant came into conflict with the upper-class Dutch of the city, called **burghers**, who wanted more rights. Despite Stuyvestant's dictatorial nature, he agreed to the establishment of a municipal government in 1653.

Under Stuyvesant, New Amsterdam grew to a population of about 8,000. Still, when the British fleet approached New Amsterdam in 1664, the leading colonists did not want to fight. Stuyvestant surrendered. New Netherland became New York, named after the Duke of York of England. There was, however, a brief period from 1673 to 1674 where the Dutch retook the colony, but they ended up returning it to Britain. Ultimately, the weakness of New Netherland was that it did not have enough of a population to compete with the British colonies in New England.

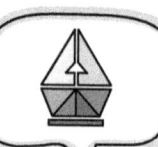
1. The Dutch were different from other European colonists in their relations with Native Americans because

    A. they did not go to war with Native Americans.

    B. they did not actively try to convert Native Americans to Christianity.

    C. they did not create any form of local self-government.

    D. they did not encourage trade or people to migrate to the colony.

2. Which of the following was a result of Kieft's War?

    A. It led to the transfer of New Netherland to Britain.

    B. It started the first municipal government in New Netherland.

    C. It resulted in the Lenape paying tribute to the Dutch.

    D. It unified Native Americans against the Dutch.

3. Who was the last Director-General of New Netherland? ....

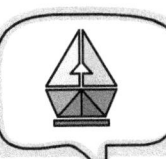
Directions: Read the text below. Then answer the questions that follow.

"

As you learned yesterday, the fundamental weakness of New Netherland was its population. At the time of the transfer of New Netherland to Britain in 1664, there were about 9,000 people living in the colony, half of which were not of Dutch descent. The neighboring British colony of Connecticut had about double that number of colonists.

The problem was that the Dutch had trouble attracting people to New Netherland. This was in part due to the prosperity and stability of the Netherlands at home. People were not as motivated to leave as they were in Britain where there was religious and civil conflict.

However, the Dutch did try to grow the colony through the use of **patroonships**. The patroon system gave a few powerful people large estates if they brought at least fifty settlers to the colony. The patroon would also be given privileges in the fur trade and the ability to create courts in their estates. The settlers would then rent out the land. Still, the colonists were under the control of the patroon. This system was unsuccessful except for the establishment of Rensselaerswyck which covered much of the area around present-day Albany, New York. Patroonships ultimately caused wealth and power to be concentrated into the hands of a few people.

New Netherland also engaged in the slave trade. Most enslaved people were purchased by the Dutch West India Company, rather than being purchased by individuals. Enslaved people built much of the colony's infrastructure, such as its roads and buildings. Slavery in New Netherland was different from in other colonies. In New Netherland, enslaved people could earn wages and many also served in the colony's militia. They were also allowed to sue colonists in court, and many won. Some became "half-slaves" after petitioning for their freedom. This meant that they were freed from bondage but still were obligated to work for the West India Company for wages. As the 1600s drew to a close, slavery became more repressive in New York as opportunities for freedom for enslaved people diminished.

"

1. In what ways did the Netherlands try to resolve the population issue in New Netherland?

....

....

....

....

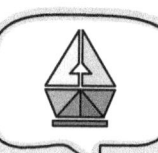
2. What may be reasons why the patroon system did not work?

....

....

....

....

3. What were the characteristics of slavery in New Netherland that made it different from slavery in other colonies?

....

....

....

....

....

Directions: Read the text below. Then answer the questions that follow.

"Although the Dutch had colonies in America for a short time, their influence on American history and culture was significant. On the surface, some of their cultural influences, such as borrowed words like "boss" seem minor, while others, such as cookies and Santa Claus may be more important. However, the Dutch fundamentally contributed to American democracy through their tradition of cultural and religious tolerance. Cultural toleration is being able to peacefully live and work with others of a different heritage. This was necessary because the New Netherland colony was so diverse. Religious toleration found its way into some of the most important political thoughts and documents of the United States, including the Bill of Rights."

1. Why is the idea of toleration important for a free society?

....

....

....

....

....

....

2. How can these ideas help to build community?

....

....

....

....

....

....

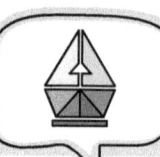
Directions: Read the text below. Then answer the questions that follow.

This week you learned about the Dutch colony in New Netherland that later became New York. You also learned the differences between New Netherland and other colonies:

1. In what ways did the New Netherland colony succeed?

....

....

....

....

....

2. Based on your study of the British colonies last week, in what ways was New Netherland similar to them?

....

....

....

....

....

3. How was the diversity of New Netherland and its capital at New Amsterdam reflective of America's history?

....

....

....

....

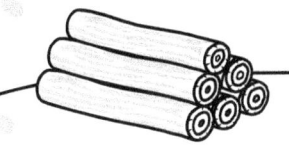

WEEK 6

Economics

The Growth of Slavery

This week, you will learn about the introduction and expansion of slavery in the American colonies. You will also learn about the conditions of the slave trade.

ARGOPREP

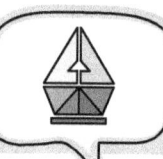
Directions: Read the text below. Then answer the questions that follow.

The growth of slavery in the American colonies was driven by a demand for labor. Slavery began as early as the 15th century when Portuguese ships, seeking wealth on the West African coast, began enslaving and trading Africans. Later, as European colonies developed in the Americas, Native Americans were also enslaved. However, Native Americans often died from diseases to which they had no immunity, which led to further enslavement of Africans. Historians date the arrival of slavery in the American colonies to 1619 when a ship carrying enslaved Africans arrived in Virginia. The practice would continue to grow over the years. Enslaved people in the Americas were primarily forced to work on large cash crop plantations, such as on sugarcane fields on islands in the Caribbean.

Slavery in the Americas was different from other forms of historical slavery. In the Americas, the colonies practiced **chattel slavery**, in which enslaved people were viewed as property, not people. This meant that, once a person was enslaved, any children that they had were also born enslaved. The treatment of enslaved people was dehumanizing and violent. Seeking reasons to justify the harsh treatment, people in power began to spread ideas that people with darker skin were inferior. These ideas spread and would later influence the racist and violent behaviors that continued even after the abolition of slavery.

Plantation owners in colonies like Virginia also relied on **indentured servants**. Indentured servants entered a contract with a planter agreeing to work for him for a certain number of years in exchange for passage to the colony, provisions, and sometimes future land. Virginia, in fact, offered **headrights** to planters who brought over indentured servants, providing 50 acres of additional land per person they brought over. Due to the harsh conditions and excessive labor, many indentured servants died before their contracts expired. As a result, plantation owners preferred the free labor of enslaved peoples. By the 1800s, the majority of labor in the colonies was being performed by enslaved peoples, with the enslavers reaping all of the profit. The practice of slavery became an integral part of the culture of the Southern colonies because of its economic importance.

1. Enslaved people's labor was used in the Americas most often for

   A. craft.

   B. trade.

   C. industry.

   D. agriculture.

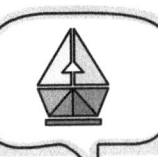
2. What are headrights?

    A. a grant of land to a planter for each indentured servant he brought into the colony

    B. a provision of land to an indentured servant upon completing his or her term

    C. a policy that enslaved Native Americans to work on plantations

    D. a practice that considered enslaved Africans to be property

3. Which of the following was a reason why the practice of slavery grew in the Americas?

    A. the use of the headright system

    B. the popularity of indentured servitude

    C. the abundance of land

    D. the desire for free labor

4. What practice ultimately led to growing racial views?

    A. colonization

    B. headrights

    C. indentured servitude

    D. chattel slavery

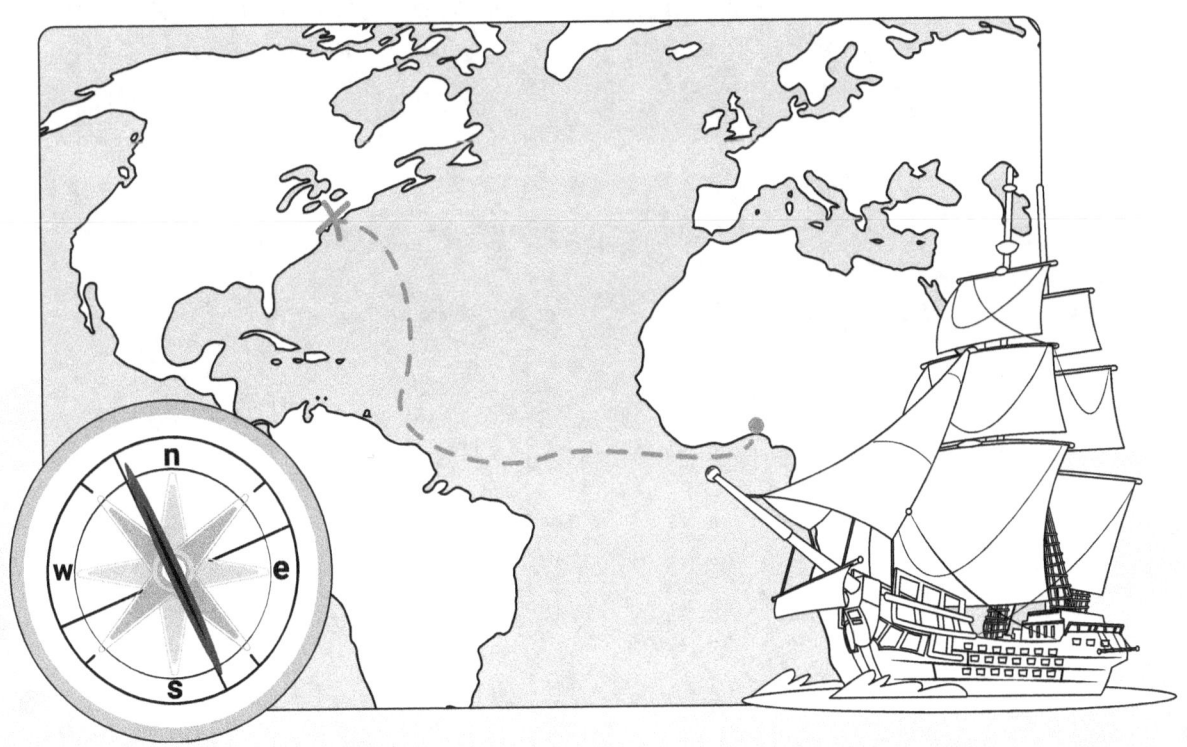

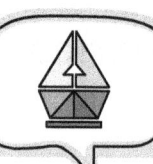
Directions: Read the text below. Then answer the questions that follow.

Slavery was a vital part of an international trade network called the **triangular trade**. The triangular trade connected three points - the Americas, Europe, and Africa, thus making a triangle.

In the Americas, ships loaded raw materials such as lumber and iron, or cash crops such as tobacco, rice and sugar and sailed for Europe. In Europe, these goods were sold and a new cargo of finished goods, alcohol, and weapons was loaded on the ships. The ships then sailed for the coast of Africa where traders would exchange that cargo with coastal tribes for enslaved people, who were often captured in war with neighboring tribes. The ship then sailed across the Atlantic to the Americas. This portion of the journey was called the **Middle Passage**. In the Americas, enslaved people were sold to plantation owners, who forced them to plant and harvest cash crops under inhumane conditions and for no pay. These raw materials were then brought to other parts of the colonies, such as New England, or to Europe where they were manufactured into finished goods.

Trade between the colonies and the practice of slavery were interconnected. Farmers in New England and the Middle Colonies grew food for plantations in the Caribbean. Other New Englanders processed Caribbean sugar into rum. Colonists who lived in colonies in which the slave trade was illegal sometimes owned or invested in property and enslaved people in other colonies. The planters of South Carolina often had connections to the Caribbean and its vast sugar plantations worked by enslaved people.

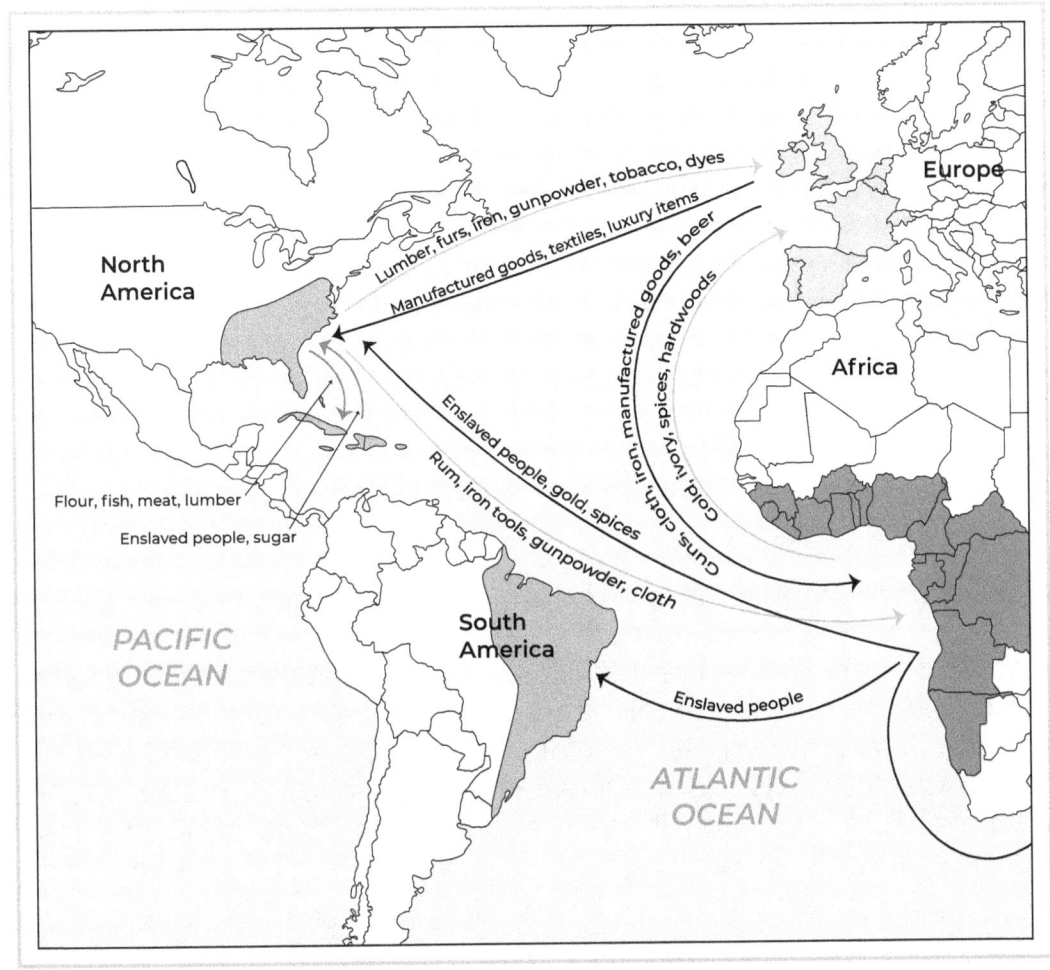

Atlantic Triangular Trade, 1500-1800s.

1. The Middle Passage was the part of the triangular trade in which

    A. raw materials were shipped from the Americas to Europe.

    B. enslaved people were transported from Africa to the Americas.

    C. finished goods were transported from Europe to Africa.

    D. cash crops were shipped from the Caribbean to North America.

2. North America was an important point in the triangular trade because it supplied

    A. raw materials.   **C.** enslaved people.

    B. finished goods   **D.** weapons.

3. What is one way that colonies in which the slave trade was illegal were still involved in the slave trade? _____

Directions: Read the text below. Then answer the questions that follow.

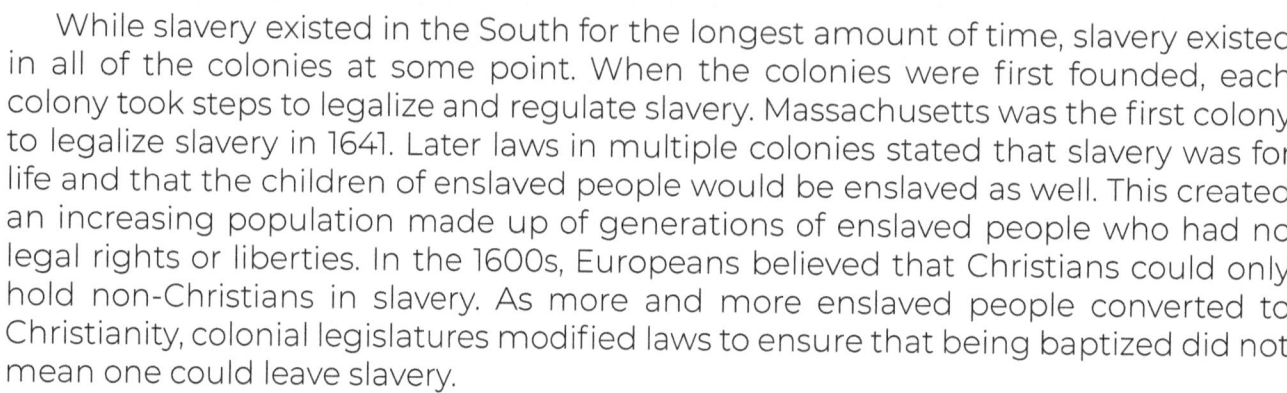

While slavery existed in the South for the longest amount of time, slavery existed in all of the colonies at some point. When the colonies were first founded, each colony took steps to legalize and regulate slavery. Massachusetts was the first colony to legalize slavery in 1641. Later laws in multiple colonies stated that slavery was for life and that the children of enslaved people would be enslaved as well. This created an increasing population made up of generations of enslaved people who had no legal rights or liberties. In the 1600s, Europeans believed that Christians could only hold non-Christians in slavery. As more and more enslaved people converted to Christianity, colonial legislatures modified laws to ensure that being baptized did not mean one could leave slavery.

While slavery was widely accepted during the colonial period, there were some objections. For example, in 1652, Rhode Island passed a law limiting the amount of time one could be a slave to ten years. This law was sidestepped by enslavers who sold the enslaved persons just as the ten years were ending and replaced them. In 1688, the Quakers of Germantown, Pennsylvania, raised objections about slavery calling it morally wrong. Most calls against slavery went unheeded. As slavery continued to grow, so did the racist views about the inferiority of enslaved people as a justification for the horrific pratice. This would become one of the great issues of American history.

1. What was the first colony to legalize slavery?

   A. Virginia

   B. South Carolina

   C. New York

   D. Massachusetts

2. What religious sect showed opposition to slavery during the colonial period?

   ....

3. How was slavery in the early colonial period partially justified?

   ....

   ....

   ....

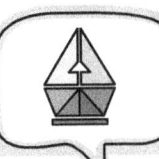
Directions: Read the text below. Then answer the questions that follow.

As you learned earlier, the Middle Passage was the part of the triangular trade where enslaved Africans were transported from Africa to the Americas on ships. Conditions were abominable. The enslaved people were chained and lived in packed quarters below decks where they could not sit or stand. With no fresh air or running water, unsanitary conditions led to disease. The voyage could take up to two months. In good weather, a captain would bring the captives on deck for exercise and feed them twice a day. Those who refused were force-fed. Those who attempted to escape by jumping overboard were punished. During the colonial period, historians estimate that about one of five enslaved people perished on the Middle Passage.

Plan of the lower deck with the stowage of 292 enslaved people.

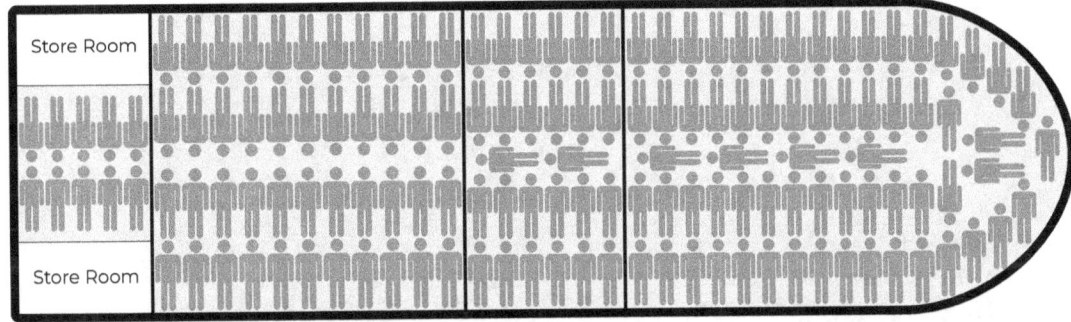

Plan of the stowage of 130 additional enslaved people on the sides of the lower deck by means of platforms or shelves.

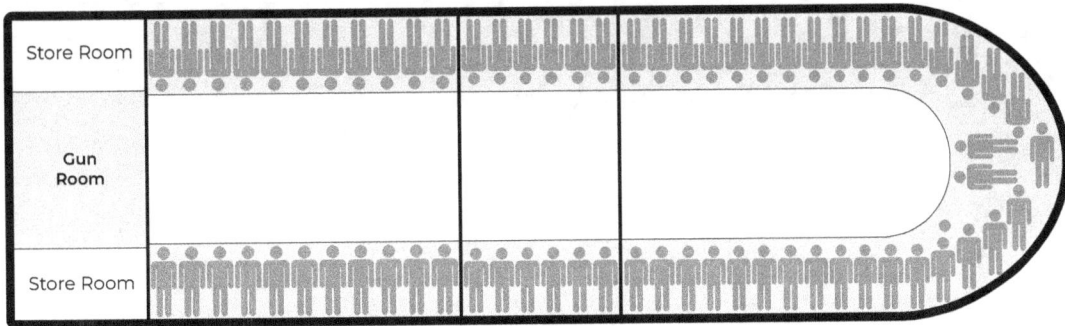

A diagram of a slave ship

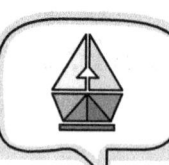
1. How might the experiences of the Middle Passage have impacted the morale of enslaved people?

....

....

....

....

....

....

2. Using the diagram from today's lesson as a guide, describe the conditions of below the decks of a slave ship in your own words.

....

....

....

....

....

....

....

....

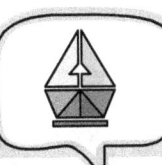
Directions: Read the text below. Then answer the questions that follow.

This week you learned about the growth of slavery in the Americas and the development of the triangular trade.

1. Describe the primary reasons for the growth of slavery in the Americas.

2. Why did racism grow simultaneously with the growth of slavery?

3. A paradox is a statement that does not agree with itself. How is slavery a paradox when compared to American ideals of democracy and liberty?

History

Causes of the American Revolution

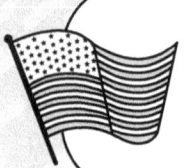

This week, you will learn about the growing tensions between Britain and the American colonies that eventually led to the American Revolution.

ARGOPREP

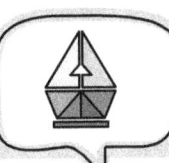
Directions: Read the text below. Then answer the questions that follow.

As you learned in Week 4, the British policy toward its American colonies was one of salutary neglect. It mostly left the colonies alone to develop as they wished. Salutary means beneficial, and for the most part the colonies thrived. The colonists remained loyal to Great Britain while at the same time learning how to govern themselves.

This was to change, however, with the **French and Indian War,** also known as the Seven Years War (1756-1763). This war was a conflict between Britain and France as well as their respective Native American allies over territory in the Americas. France lost the war and had to give Canada to Britain. This was considered to be a major victory for not just Britain but for the American colonies who were rivals of the French colonies.

The war, however, laid the seeds for future troubles. Britain was put under enormous strain due to the war and wanted to avoid future conflicts with other colonies and Native Americans. It issued the **Proclamation of 1763** which forbade colonists to settle west of the Appalachian Mountains and stated that only the British government could make treaties with Native American tribes. Native Americans had been growing hostile to colonists since more of them were pushing west into their territory. American colonists hated the Proclamation since it limited their ability to expand westward.

The war also left Britain badly in debt. It needed to raise revenue. Members of **Parliament**, the British legislature, reasoned that since the colonies received protection from their military they should be responsible to help pay for some of the expenses of the war. This viewpoint would lead to more laws that would inflame the colonies.

North America after the French and Indian War

Boundary between Mississippi River and 49th parallel uncertain due to misconception that source of Mississippi River lay further north

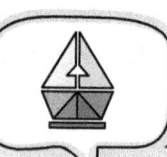
1. The French and Indian war resulted in

    A. independence for the American colonies.

    B. the French control of Canada.

    C. the expansion of British power.

    D. more land for colonists.

2. Why did the British government enact the Proclamation of 1763?

    A. to raise revenue for the British government.

    B. to provide a buffer between the colonies and French Canada.

    C. to secure more natural resources for the American colonies.

    D. to appease Native American tribes to the west.

3. Why did American colonists dislike the Proclamation of 1763?

    A. It resulted in higher taxation.

    B. It gave land to rival colonists.

    C. It cut off the trade in enslaved persons.

    D. It limited their ability to expand westward.

4. What problem was a result of the French and Indian War?

    A. British war debt

    B. American colonial rebellion

    C. British military losses

    D. American colonial economic collapse

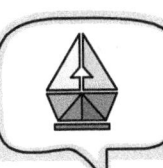
Directions: Read the text below. Then answer the questions that follow.

As you learned yesterday, the French and Indian War cost Britain a lot of money. This led to a great amount of debt for the British government. To pay back their debt, they enacted new taxation laws on their American colonies. This caused resentment in the colonies which broke out into violence and in turn resulted in other laws that the colonists viewed as repressive. The colonists did not have any representatives in Parliament, so they had no say on these laws or taxes. Colonists said these laws were unfair, stating, "No taxation without representation!" These events would eventually push the American colonies to fight for their independence. Some of the major tax acts of Parliament are outlined in the table below:

Year	Law	What it Did
1764	**The Sugar Act**	Placed taxes on sugar and molasses and raised taxes on silk, wine, coffee, pimento, and indigo. This was later modified in 1766.
1765	**The Stamp Act**	Placed a tax on most printed materials. After massive colonial resistance, the act was repealed in 1766.
1766	**The Declaratory Act**	After Parliament repealed the Stamp Act and changed the Sugar Act to appease the colonies, it passed this law which declared that it had the right to tax the colonies.
1767	**The Townshend Acts**	These were a series of laws that placed taxes on various goods imported into the colonies such as paper, paint, glass, lead, china, and tea. It also gave extended powers to enforce the new taxes. This resulted in massive protests, boycotts, and a declaration by the Virginia House of Burgesses that only it could tax Virginians. The Massachusetts Assembly was dissolved because it refused to enforce the acts.
1773	**The Tea Act**	This act gave the East India Company a monopoly on tea sales to the colonies. Colonial tea merchants were worried this would drive them out of business. This resulted in the dumping of 342 chests of tea into Boston Harbor during a protest called the "Boston Tea Party."

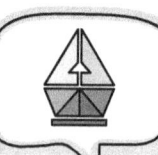
Year	Law	What it Did
1774	**The Coercive Acts**	The Coercive Acts were a series of laws meant to punish Massachusetts and force the colonies to accept Parliament's authority. They closed the Port of Boston and revoked the Massachusetts colonial charter. These acts were called the "Intolerable Acts" by the colonists.

1. Which of the following put a tax on most printed material?

    A. the Coercive Acts

    B. the Stamp Act

    C. the Declaratory Act

    D. the Townshend Acts

2. Through what law did Parliament assert that it had the power to tax the colonies?

    A. the Tea Act.

    B. the Declaratory Act

    C. the Sugar Act

    D. the Stamp Act

3. What was the main objection of colonists to Parliament's efforts to raise revenue?

    A. The colonies had their own colonial legislatures that were responsible for taxation.

    B. The colonies would suffer economically through the implementation of taxes.

    C. The colonies did not support the French and Indian War and therefore the taxes were illegal.

    D. The colonies needed to have representation in Parliament for taxes to be legitimate.

4. The Boston Tea Party was in response to

    A. a new tax designed to raise revenue.

    B. a granting of a monopoly to the East India Company.

    C. colonial objections to the Stamp Act.

    D. a declaration by Parliament that they had authority to tax.

Directions: Read the text below. Then answer the questions that follow.

"

Colonial objections to Parliament's taxes can be explained by seeing how the perspective on politics and government evolved during the 17th and 18th centuries throughout the **Enlightenment**. The Enlightenment was an intellectual movement that emphasized reason. Writers, such as John Locke, emphasized natural rights -the belief that people were born with certain rights that they could not lose such as life, liberty, and property. Locke also emphasized that governments only had power through the "consent of the governed." This meant that if a government was abusing its power then that government was no longer legitimate.

It was the force of those ideas that brought the colonies together. In 1754, before the French and Indian War, Benjamin Franklin proposed at a conference in Albany, New York that they should unite the colonies in what was called the **Albany Plan of Union**. This plan was not adopted. In 1765, representatives from nine colonies created the **Stamp Act Congress** to protest taxation without representation as an abuse of British authority. As the situation grew more volatile, the colonies moved to form **committees of correspondence** to keep one another informed about British activities. Then in 1774, twelve colonies formed the **First Continental Congress** to debate whether they could peacefully resolve the situation with Britain or to fight. They issued a **Declaration of Rights and Grievances** stating that they were loyal to the King but condemned the Intolerable Acts. They agreed to meet the next year for the **Second Continental Congress** if no resolution was reached. This congress established an army headed by George Washington. Fighting broke out and on July 4, 1776 the Continental Congress approved the **Declaration of Independence.** Written primarily by Thomas Jefferson, the Declaration backed natural rights and the consent of the governed. It stated that because of the abuses of power by Parliament, the colonies were now independent from Britain and would become the United States.

"

1. What was the purpose of the committees of correspondence?

    A. to provide for a colonial army

    B. to protest the Stamp Act

    C. to keep colonies informed on British activities

    D. to promote the ideas of John Locke

2. Which is an example of a natural right proposed by John Locke?

    A. property   **C.** livelihood

    B. speech   **D.** religion

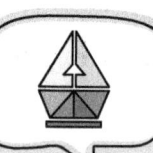
3. Who proposed the Albany Plan of Union?

    A. George Washington

    B. John Locke

    C. Benjamin Franklin

    D. Thomas Jefferson

4. What occurred at the First Continental Congress?

....

....

....

....

....

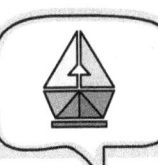
Directions: Read the text below. Then answer the questions that follow.

The following passage is an excerpt from the *Declaration of Independence*:

"We hold these truths to be self-evident, that all men are created equal, that they are endowed by their Creator with certain unalienable Rights, that among these are Life, Liberty and the pursuit of Happiness. - That to secure these rights, Governments are instituted among Men, deriving their just powers from the consent of the governed, - That whenever any Form of Government becomes destructive of these ends, it is the Right of the People to alter or to abolish it, and to institute new Government, laying its foundation on such principles and organizing its powers in such form, as to them shall seem most likely to effect their Safety and Happiness."

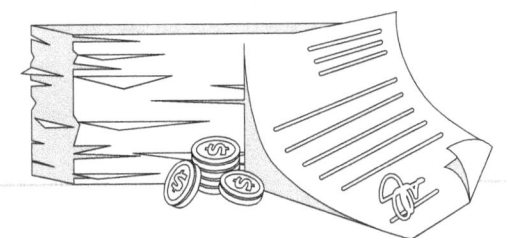

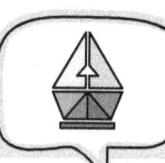
1. What is the purpose of government according the Declaration of Independence? Use your own words.

....

....

....

2. When the Declaration of Independence states "whenever any Form of Government becomes destructive of these ends" what is it referring to?

....

....

....

....

....

3. How is the Declaration of Independence relevant to you today?

....

....

....

....

....

Directions: Read the text below. Then answer the questions that follow.

This week you learned about the causes of the American Revolution that led to the Declaration of Independence.

1. How did the colonies' views of themselves change over time?

2. How is the notion of "taxation without representation" linked to the ideals of the Declaration of Independence?

3. Do you think that the situation leading up to the Declaration of Independence could have been avoided? How might the colonies have stayed under British control?

History

The War of Independence

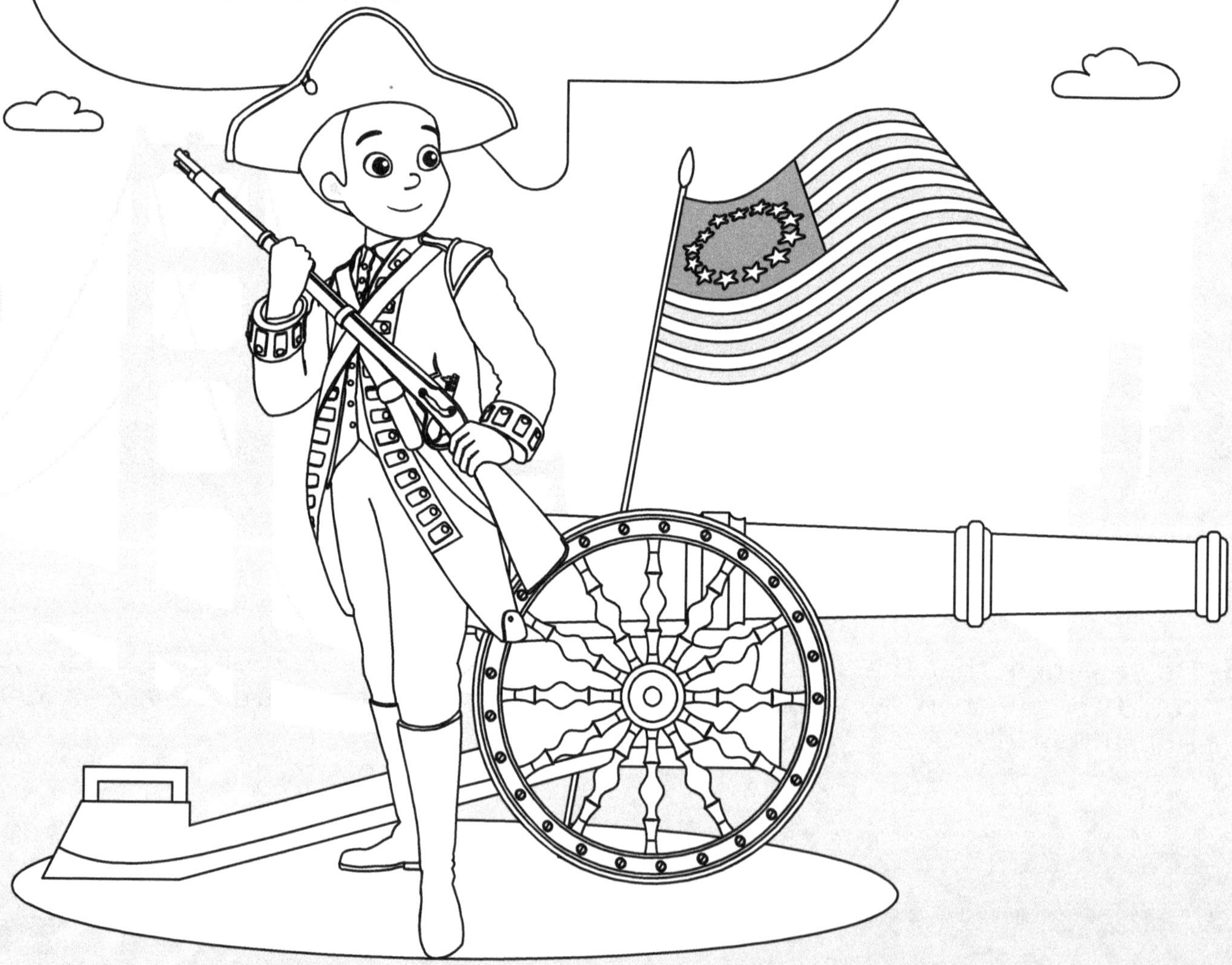

This week, you will learn about the Revolutionary War and how the colonists fought successfully for independence in a struggle that lasted eight years.

ARGOPREP

Directions: Read the text below. Then answer the questions that follow.

The American Revolutionary War, or the American War of Independence, lasted from 1775 to 1783. The British and the American forces each had their strengths and weaknesses:

	Strengths	Weaknesses
British	• Military experience • Economic strength • Strong naval forces	• Fighting far from home • Some troops were hired to fight and did not have strong morale
Americans	• Familiar with the land • Leadership • Foreign support	• No central government • Material shortages • Lack of training

The American forces had considerably less experience than the British forces. Also, they lacked war materials and faced shortages not only of arms and ammunition but of food. Still, the Americans had a key advantage of fighting on their own territory and a key leader in the general of the Continental Army, George Washington. Washington managed to keep the morale of his forces high even as they lost several key battles.

In the end, the key to American victory was the support of the French government. France was the first country to recognize the United States as independent in 1778. Its support brought about key victories that ended the war in 1783.

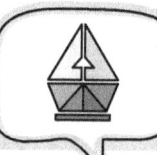
1. A strength of the British military during the Revolutionary War was
   A. foreign support.
   B. familiarity with the territory.
   C. military experience.
   D. leadership.

2. What was a weakness of the American army during the Revolutionary War?
   A. untrained troops
   B. unfamiliarity with the terrain
   C. low morale
   D. poor leadership

3. What was a key reason why the Americans won the Revolutionary War?
   A. naval power
   B. foreign assistance
   C. economic strength
   D. better weapons

4. Why would the lack of a central government be a weakness for the Americans fighting the Revolutionary War?
   A. There would be less popular support for independence.
   B. There would be difficulty making quick decisions.
   C. There would be less talented people.
   D. There would be too powerful a control structure.

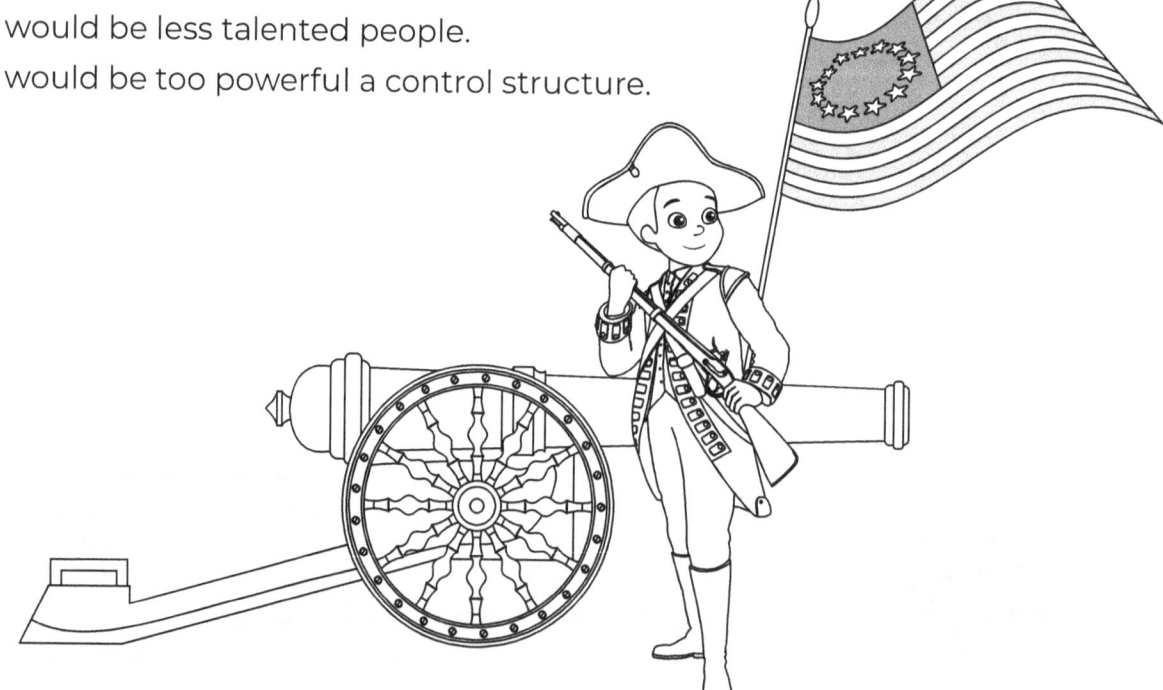

Directions: Read the text below. Then answer the questions that follow.

The Revolutionary War consisted of many battles. These battles pitted the Continental Army against the British. The British were also supported by a number of colonists who did not want independence. These people were called **loyalists** or **tories**. Those who wanted independence were called **patriots**. This timeline describes the major battles of the Revolutionary War and its results.

Date	Battle	Description
April 19, 1775	**Battles of Lexington and Concord**	These small battles between British redcoats and Patriot minutemen were really skirmishes and marked the start of fighting in the war. It was a Patriot victory.
June 17, 1775	**Battle of Bunker Hill**	This was the first major battle of the war. It was fought mainly near Boston on Breed's Hill with Bunker Hill nearby. It resulted in a British victory but only after heavy losses. It showed that the rebels could stand up to British forces.
April 27, 1776	**Battle of Long Island**	Fought in Brooklyn, New York, this battle is also called the Battle of Brooklyn. It was a Patriot loss and resulted in the British, under the command of General William Howe, taking control of New York City.

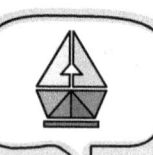
Date	Battle	Description
December 25, 1776	Battle of Trenton	This battle was a surprise attack led by George Washington across the Delaware River against British mercenary forces in Trenton, New Jersey. This battle was a great success and helped to build up American morale in the face of losses.
September 19 and October 7, 1777	First and Second Battles of Saratoga	These two battles fought in Saratoga saw decisive victories by patriot forces led by General Horatio Gates over British General John Burgoyne. This battle convinced France to support the American cause and was a turning point in the war.
October 19, 1781	Battle of Yorktown	Also called the Siege of Yorktown, American forces led by George Washington and French forces surrounded the British army, led by British General Lord Charles Cornwallis. The British surrendered, marking the end of hostilities.

While the Battle of Yorktown was the final major battle in the Revolutionary War, the Treaty of Paris, which formalized the end of the conflict, was not formally adopted until September 3, 1783.

1. Which battle resulted in a British victory but only after heavy losses?
   A. Battle of Yorktown
   B. Battle of Bunker Hill
   C. Battle of Trenton
   D. Battle of Long Island

2. Which event marked a turning point in the war in the Americans favor?
   A. Battle of Long Island
   B. Battle of Trenton
   C. Battles of Lexington and Concord
   D. Battles of Saratoga

3. Which general led the American forces at the Battles of Saratoga?
   A. Charles Cornwallis
   B. John Burgoyne
   C. Horatio Gates
   D. George Washington

4. Who led a surprise attack against Hessian forces in Trenton, New Jersey on December 25, 1776?
   A. George Washington
   B. Horatio Gates
   C. William Howe
   D. Charles Cornwallis

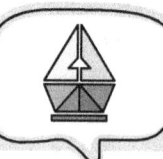
Directions: Read the text below. Then answer the questions that follow.

In the Declaration of Independence, Native Americans were described as "the merciless Indian Savages, whose known Rule of Warfare, is an undistinguished Destruction, of all Ages, Sexes and Conditions." Meanwhile, the British Proclamation of 1763 stopped colonial settlement west of the Appalachian Mountains. Native Americans were concerned that an independent United States would soon push them out of their lands. Still, some Native American groups sided with the colonies. Others sided with the British, and many tried to remain neutral.

One divided Native American group was the Iroquois Confederacy. The Mohawk leader, **Joseph Brant** maintained an alliance with Britain and drew in the Seneca, Onondaga, and Cayuga. The Oneida and the Tuscarora sided with the Americans. This led to civil war among the Iroquois which was made worse by American attacks through Iroquois territory in 1779.

The majority of Native American tribes did side with the British by the end of the war. The resulting **Treaty of Paris** gave land to the United States with no regard to the Native Americans who inhabited it. Ultimately, the view of Native Americans revealed in the Declaration of Independence, coupled with many of the tribes siding with the British, explains in part why the United States government had few qualms about taking their lands.

1. Who was Joseph Brant?

   A. a Mohawk leader who sided with the British

   B. a British ambassador to the Iroquois

   C. a colonial officer who attacked Native Americans

   D. a Native American chief who tried to remain neutral

2. During the Revolutionary War, Native American tribes were most concerned with

   A. their natural rights.

   B. their ability to trade.

   C. their relations with other tribes.

   D. the status of their lands.

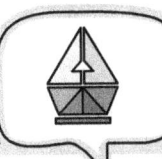
3. What was the perspective on Native Americans as written in the Declaration of Independence?

    A. that they were to be enslaved

    B. that they were useful allies

    C. that they were entitled to rights

    D. that they were savages

4. How did the Treaty of Paris impact Native Americans?

....

....

....

....

....

....

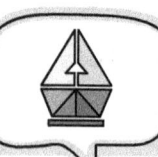
Directions: Read the text below. Then answer the questions that follow.

The map below shows the United States after the Treaty of Paris in 1783.

Results of the revelution - Treaty of Paris in 1783

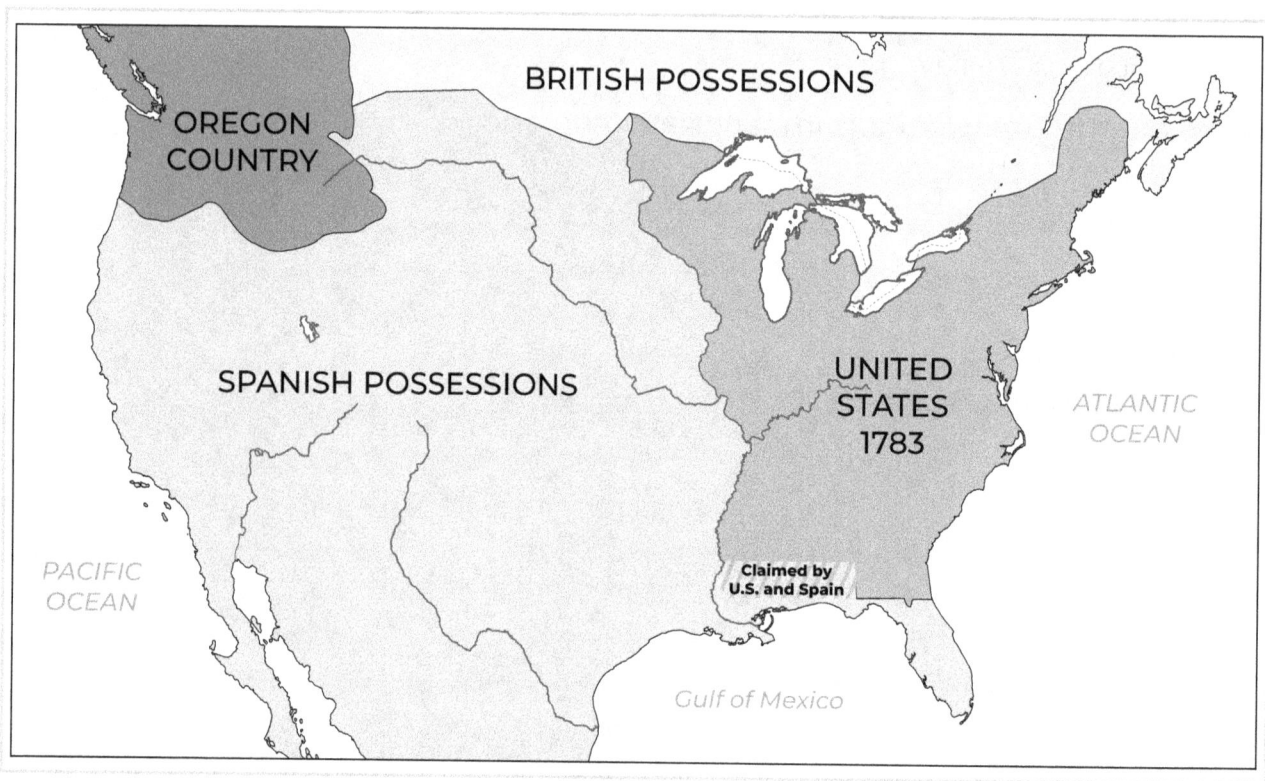

1. Which other countries' territories border the United States?

   ....

2. Take a look at the map of the American colonies from Week 7. What changes have occurred between the two maps?

   ....

   ....

3. Examine a current map of the United States. How is that map different?

   ....

   ....

Directions: Read the text below. Then answer the questions that follow.

This week you learned about Revolutionary War and the Treaty of Paris that resulted in the creation of the new United States of America.

1. How might the victory at the Battles of Saratoga have helped to convince the French to join the American cause?

....

....

....

....

2. If you were a leader of a Native American tribe, what stance toward the Revolutionary War would you take? Elaborate on your reasoning.

....

....

....

....

3. George Washington is celebrated for his role in the Revolutionary War. What was his role and why was it so critical?

....

....

....

....

....

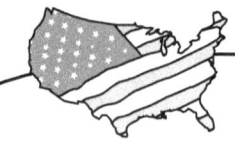

Civics and Government

America Under the Articles of Confederation

This week, you will learn about the Articles of Confederation, the first constitution of the United States, and the problems the country faced in its early years.

ARGOPREP

Directions: Read the text below. Then answer the questions that follow.

A **constitution** is a written document that provides the overall framework and laws of government. The first constitution of the United States was the **Articles of Confederation**. The Articles were first adopted during the War of Independence in 1777 and were not approved by all states until 1781.

At that time, individual states such as Massachusetts, Virginia, and New York looked at themselves as being independent from the other states. In fact, in many ways each individual state looked at itself as its own unique country. As a result, the Articles of Confederation set up a weak central government. Under the Articles, there was a national Congress that could approve treaties and settle disputes between states. It could also declare war against other countries and raise arms. Yet that was the entire government. There were no national courts or head executives like the president. The states ruled themselves.

State **sovereignty**, or the right to rule oneself, was considered to be of chief importance. Each state had one vote in Congress and laws could only be passed if nine of the thirteen states agreed. The central government lacked key powers such as the power to tax or regulate trade. In order to raise revenue, Congress could only ask the states for money. Individual states had the power to impose separate tariffs, or taxes on imported goods, which created trade wars between states. As a result, the early United States had a troubled economy and a weak government.

1. What is a power that Congress had under the Articles of Confederation?

   A. to regulate trade

   B. to impose tariffs

   C. to tax

   D. to approve treaties

2. How would you compare the national government and the state governments under the Articles of Confederation?

   A. The national government was weaker than the state governments.

   B. The national government was stronger than the state governments.

   C. The national government was equal in power to the state governments.

   D. The national government was sovereign and the state governments were not.

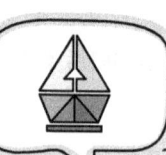
3. What is sovereignty?

    A. the power to tax

    B. the right to rule oneself

    C. the ability to approve treaties

    D. the structure of government

4. How was the idea of state power maintained in the national Congress under the Articles of Confederation?

    A. Each state had the power to declare war.

    B. Any state could negotiate a treaty.

    C. Any state could veto a law.

    D. Each state had one vote.

Directions: Read the text below. Then answer the questions that follow.

Despite the weaknesses of the Articles of Confederation, the government of the United States did have some successes in its early years. It promoted trade with foreign nations through new treaties. It also managed lands in the west. While Congress could not tax, it did raise some revenue by organizing and selling lands west of the Appalachian Mountains, despite there being Native Americans already there. Congress first passed the **Land Ordinance of 1785** which arranged these western territories into townships. In 1787, Congress passed the **Northwest Ordinance**. This law created the **Northwest Territory** which was the area north of the Ohio River and east of the Mississippi River. This larger territory was later divided into smaller territories. When each territory reached a population of 60,000 it could then apply for statehood. Once a state, that territory would be equal to the other states. The Northwest Ordinance also banned slavery within the Northwest territory. In the future, slavery would remain legal in the southern states and illegal in the northern states.

The Northwest Territory showing when its territories were given statehood.

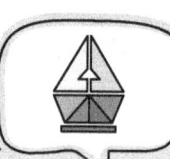
1. Which territory in the Northwest Territory became a state first?

    A. Ohio

    B. Michigan

    C. Indiana

    D. Minnesota

2. What did the Northwest Ordinance do about slavery in the Northwest Territory?

    A. It let states decide.

    B. It let people vote on it.

    C. It required it.

    D. It banned it.

3. What is one way Congress raised revenue?

    A. It imposed tariffs.

    B. It taxed individual citizens.

    C. It taxed the states.

    D. It sold land west of the Appalachians.

4. Why was the Northwest Ordinance important for the future growth of the United States?

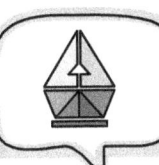
Directions: Read the text below. Then answer the questions that follow.

Under the Articles of Confederation, the young United States experienced many problems. One of the worst problems was a **recession**, which is a severe economic downturn. Part of the reason for this downturn was because the federal government as well as the individual states had a lot of debt from fighting the Revolutionary War. Some states even turned to printing paper money to pay debts. This resulted in inflation, which is the decrease in value of money and an increase in the price of goods. In 1786, the Massachusetts State Legislature decided not to print more money but instead to raise taxes. In response to this increase in taxes, **Daniel Shays**, a bankrupt farmer and Revolutionary War veteran, led a rebellion of struggling farmers in western Massachusetts. They claimed they were being ignored by the state and seized an arsenal, which is a place where the military kept its weapons. **Shays' Rebellion**, as it was called, was eventually stopped by the military, but not before it demonstrated the weakness of the central government.

Shays' Rebellion made wealthier Americans worried. They feared that without a strong central government and a strong military, the states might start to listen to the demands of their less wealthy citizens, redistributing wealth and land more fairly. They grew to believe that a stronger form of government was needed and that the Articles of Confederation needed to be changed or replaced.

1. Who was Daniel Shays?
   A. a bankrupt farmer who objected to taxes
   B. a wealthy landholder who supported a rebellion
   C. a general who put down a rebellion
   D. a governor who printed money to pay debts

2. What was a cause of inflation after the Revolutionary War?
   A. bad diplomatic relations
   B. states printing money
   C. poorer citizens causing disruptions
   D. local governments raising taxes

3. What problem did many states have after the Revolutionary War?
   A. weak governments
   B. ineffective militaries
   C. large debts
   D. falling prices

4. Explain how Shays' Rebellion caused upper class people to reconsider the Articles of Confederation?

....

....

....

Directions: Read the text below. Then answer the questions that follow.

An ongoing theme in American history is the debate between having a central government that is too strong versus one that is too weak. This week, you have learned about the problems of having a weak central government.

1. What might be some benefits of having a government that does not have much power?

2. Governments today serve many functions. Write a list of what you think the four most important functions of government are.

3. What level of power do you think is appropriate for a government to have? What if it is too strong? What if it is too weak?

Directions: Read the text below. Then answer the questions that follow.

This week you learned about America's first constitution, the Articles of Confederation. You also learned of problems with the Articles and how it inspired calls for change.

1. Which functions of the Articles of Confederation might have been useful during the Revolutionary War?

_____

_____

_____

_____

_____

_____

2. How did state sovereignty work with the Articles of Confederation?

_____

_____

_____

_____

_____

_____

3. Why did the Articles of Confederation fail to create a strong and successful nation? Support your answer with at least one example from the readings.

_____

_____

_____

_____

_____

_____

WEEK 10

Civics and Government

The Creation of the Constitution

This week, you will learn about the Constitutional Convention and the debates that shaped the federal government of today.

ARGOPREP

Directions: Read the text below. Then answer the questions that follow.

In 1787, American leaders decided that the Articles of Confederation needed to be changed. Fifty-five delegates from twelve of the thirteen states met in Philadelphia in what was called the **Constitutional Convention**. Only Rhode Island did not attend. George Washington presided over the meetings.

It soon became obvious to the delegates that the Articles needed to be replaced entirely by a new constitution. This new plan was proposed by James Madison of Virginia in the **Virginia Plan**. The Virginia Plan became the blueprint for the United States **Constitution**, which is still in use today.

The Constitution created a new **federal**, or national, government for the United States, divided into three branches. The first was the **legislative branch**, whose job was to create the laws. The second was the **executive branch**, headed by a president, whose job was to enforce the laws. The third was the **judicial branch**, a national court system of which the Supreme Court was chief.

While there was general agreement among the delegates on the creation of the three branches of government, there was disagreement on the details. One important debate was over how the legislative branch would be shaped. In Madison's Virginia Plan, he proposed a **bicameral**, or two-house, legislature called **Congress**, made up of a Senate and a House of Representatives. In this plan, the number of legislators would be chosen based on the population of a state. The more people who lived in a state, the more legislators they would have.

Smaller states did not like this plan since they felt that it would only benefit states with large populations. William Patterson offered the **New Jersey Plan**, which proposed to have a one-house legislature where every state had the same amount of representatives. After intense debate, Roger Sherman of Connecticut worked out the **Great Compromise** in which the number of representatives in the House of Representatives would be based on each state's population, while the Senate would have an equal number of representatives for each state.

Another debate erupted over the issue of slavery. Southern states wanted enslaved people counted as a part of their population. States in the North, which had fewer enslaved people, objected stating that enslaved people did not have rights. In the end, the Convention worked out the **Three-Fifths Compromise**, in which every five enslaved persons would count as three free persons for representation.

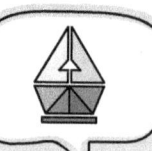
1. Who proposed the Virginia Plan?

   A. William Patterson

   B. Roger Sherman

   C. George Washington

   D. James Madison

2. What is the role of the executive branch of government?

   A. to create laws

   B. to head the congress

   C. to head the court system

   D. to enforce the laws

3. What was the issue that resulted in the Great Compromise?

   A. powers of the president

   B. representation in Congress

   C. counting enslaved persons

   D. number of branches of government

4. What leads the judicial branch of government?

   A. the Supreme Court

   B. the House of Representatives

   C. the President

   D. the Senate

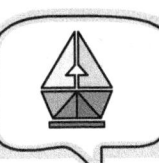
Directions: Read the text below. Then answer the questions that follow.

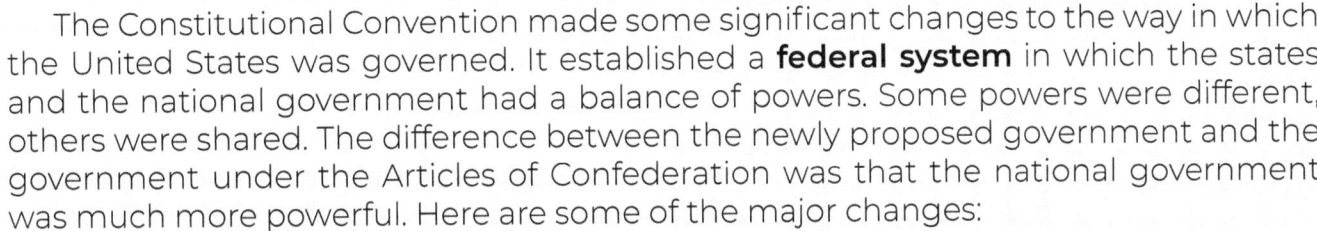

The Constitutional Convention made some significant changes to the way in which the United States was governed. It established a **federal system** in which the states and the national government had a balance of powers. Some powers were different, others were shared. The difference between the newly proposed government and the government under the Articles of Confederation was that the national government was much more powerful. Here are some of the major changes:

* There was now an executive branch headed by a president, elected by the citizens, who guided foreign policy, appointed judges, led the military, and vetoed laws. Under the articles, there had been a president of Congress elected yearly from its membership.

* There was now a judicial branch overseeing federal law. Before, state courts handled disputes, and the Congress under the Articles resolved disputes between states.

* Congress now had the power to levy taxes. Before, only states could levy taxes - this was a weakness of the Articles.

* Congress could now regulate trade between the United States and other countries, as well as between states. Before, Congress could only regulate foreign trade.

The United States was to be a **democratic republic** where citizens elected leaders to represent them. Even though at this point in the country's history, only white males owning property could vote, it was a radical idea in an age where many countries were still ruled by monarchies.

When the Constitutional Convention was over, nine of the thirteen states needed to approve, or **ratify**, the new Constitution in order for it to become law. The newly proposed federal government was much more powerful and states would lose much of their sovereignty if they approved it. A hot debate was to come.

1. What is a federal system of government?

   A. a government led by a single authority or ruler who listens to the advice of others

   B. a government in which state sovereignty is protected and a national government is weaker

   C. a government in which both states and a national government have different and shared powers

   D. a government in which all citizens vote

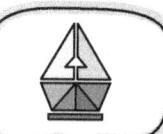
2. The new American system of government under the Constitution was radical for its time because

    A. it was a democracy.

    B. it was a monarchy.

    C. it had a strong central government.

    D. it restricted voting.

3. How did the power of regulating trade change with the Constitution over the Articles of Confederation?

    A. It gave Congress the power to control foreign trade.

    B. It gave Congress the power to tax.

    C. It gave Congress the power to regulate trade between states.

    D. It gave Congress the power to enforce regulations.

4. Why would states be concerned about the powers of the proposed Constitution?

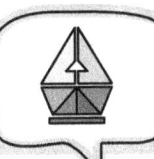
Directions: Read the text below. Then answer the questions that follow.

In order for the Constitution to become law, nine of the thirteen states needed to ratify it. People split into two camps. Those who backed ratifying the Constitution called themselves **Federalists**. Those who were against the Constitution were called the **Anti-Federalists**.

The Anti-Federalists admitted that the Articles of Confederation needed to be replaced but were concerned about the national government becoming so powerful that the individual states would lose their rights and powers. Major Anti-Federalists included George Clinton of New York, John Hancock, Samuel Adams, George Mason and Patrick Henry. They were aware that the United States had just fought a war to end monarchy and did not want a government so powerful that it would take individual liberties away.

Alexander Hamilton, John Jay, and James Madison who were some of the leading Federalists, responded to the Anti-Federalist concerns in a series of essays. They emphasized that the system of government under the Constitution was a federal one where power was divided between the national and state governments. The states would retain important powers. They argued that dividing power between a strong national government and state governments was in the best interest of the country. Their collection of essays, called the **Federalist Papers**, is an important set of documents in American history.

The Anti-Federalists were not convinced and wanted to include a **Bill of Rights** which protected individual liberties. The Federalists agreed and the first ten amendments to the Constitution, which protect individual liberties, are called the Bill of Rights. The Constitution was ratified and the new government went into effect on March 4, 1789, with George Washington as the country's first president.

1. What was a main concern of the Anti-Federalists?

    A. individual rights and liberties

    B. a weak national government

    C. that the Constitution would not be ratified

    D. that the Articles of Confederation were ending

2. Who was a prominent Federalist?

    A. Samuel Adams   **C.** Patrick Henry

    B. Alexander Hamilton   **D.** George Mason

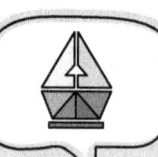
3. What document was a compromise between the Anti-Federalists and the federalists?

....

4. How did the Federalists try to sooth Anti-Federalist fears?

....

....

....

....

....

....

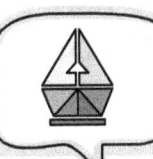
Directions: Read the text below. Then answer the questions that follow.

The signing of the U.S. Constitution

The Great Compromise shaped the Congress of today. In the Senate, states are equally represented by two senators. In the House, the number of representatives is determined by population. Some people debate this and state that Congress isn't democratic, meaning all people do not have the same voice or power.

1. Look up the population of your state. Then, look up how many representatives your state has in the House. Next, look up the population of a neighboring state, as well as the number of representatives they have in the House. Describe your findings below.

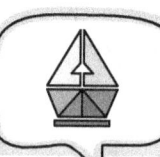

2. What might be an argument supporting the idea that each state has equal representation in Congress?

....

....

....

3. How do you think states should be represented in Congress? Do you agree with the way Congress is structured in the Constitution?

....

....

....

Directions: Read the text below. Then answer the questions that follow.

This week you learned about the creation of the United States Constitution and its ratification. You also learned about the debates that shaped the current system of American government.

1. What were the main debates at the Constitutional Convention over?

_____

_____

_____

2. What did the Three-Fifth's Compromise accomplish? What issue was this over?

_____

_____

_____

3. Do you think that the concerns of the Anti-Federalists were valid fears?

_____

_____

_____

_____

_____

Civics and Government

You and the Constitution

IN GOD WE TRUST

This week, you will learn about the separation of powers and the checks and balances of the U.S. Constitution. You will also learn about the Bill of Rights.

ARGOPREP

Directions: Read the text below. Then answer the questions that follow.

The U.S.Constitution was ratified in 1788 and took effect in 1789. After the Constitution was ratified, ten amendments were added to it called the **Bill of Rights**, which protects the individual liberties of citizens. The Constitution created the system of government that is still in use in America today. This system includes **checks and balances** so that no single part of government becomes too powerful. Each branch of government has different powers. This is called a **separation of powers**. The chart below shows how these powers are divided and used to keep each of the branches in check.

Branch and Powers		
Executive (President)	**Legislative (Congress)**	**Judicial (Supreme Court)**
* Enforces the laws * Commander-in-Chief of Armed Forces * Appoints Ambassadors and Officials * Manages foreign policy	* Creates laws * Approves Presidential appointments * Declares war * Levies taxes * Regulates trade * Approves treaties	* Interprets the Constitution * Rules on decisions of lower courts * Determines if laws are fair

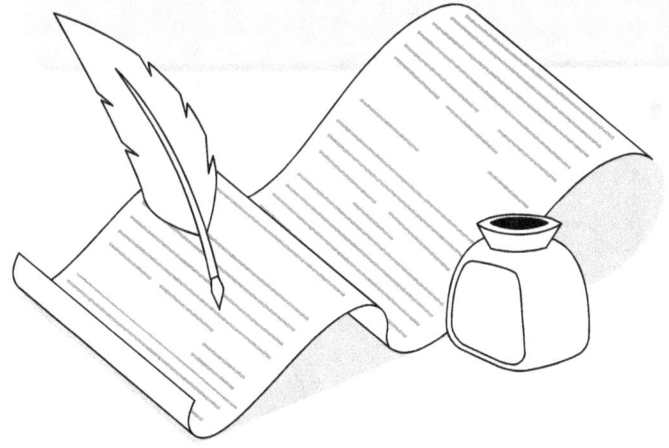

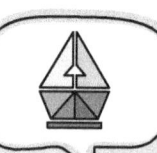
	Check on Executive Branch	Check on Legislative Branch	Check on Judicial Branch
Executive (President)		* Can veto (reject) laws	* Nominates new justices
Legislative (Congress)	* Can override a veto with a two-thirds majority * Can impeach and remove presidents * Can reject treaties * Can reject appointments		* Can impeach and remove Supreme Court Justices * Can reject Supreme Court nominations
Judicial (Supreme Court)	* Can declare a presidential action unconstitutional	* Can declare a law unconstitutional	

1. What is a check that Congress has over the President?

   A. can veto laws

   B. can make appointments

   C. can impeach

   D. can declare actions unconstitutional

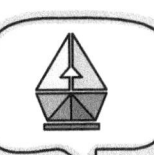
2. What is a power of the Supreme Court?

   A. to create laws

   B. to interpret the law

   C. to head the armed forces

   D. to levy taxes

3. What is a check the executive branch has over the legislative branch?

   A. can ratify treaties

   B. can declare laws unconstitutional

   C. veto power

   D. impeachment power

4. What is the purpose of separation of powers and checks and balances in the Constitution?

   A. to prevent tyranny

   B. to make quick decisions

   C. to encourage a strong economy

   D. to promote a powerful government

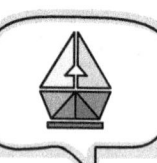
Directions: Read the text below. Then answer the questions that follow.

Let's take a deeper look into how the Constitution works by studying how a bill becomes a law. Laws originate in the Senate or House of Representatives and then are either signed into law by the president or vetoed. While this process may seem straightforward, there is much happening behind the scenes. This chart shows how complex the legislative process is.

A person comes up with an idea for a law. This can be members of Congress, the president, and citizens.

The proposal for the law is introduced by a member of Congress in either the House of Representatives or Senate

The bill is discussed in Congressional committees in areas that pertain to the subject of the bill. Hearings, study, and debate may occur.

The bill is then debated on the floor in the part of Congress where it originated. Amendments are added.

A vote is taken. If the bill passes it goes to the other chamber of Congress where it is debated, amended, and voted on.

Once a bill passes both chambers of Congress, it is amended by a **conference committee** so that the final draft of the bill is acceptable.

The bill is then forwarded to the President. The President may:

Sign the bill and it becomes law.

Veto the bill and reject it.

*   Congress may choose to **override** the veto with a two-thirds majority and then the bill becomes a law. This is rare - only about five percent of vetoes have been overridden in American history.

Do nothing

*   If ten days pass and Congress is still in session, the bill **becomes a law.**
*   If ten days pass and Congress is out of session, the bill does not become a law. This is called a **pocket veto.**

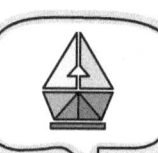
1. When Congress goes out of session after passing a bill and the president does not sign the bill, what happens?

   A. the entire process restarts

   B. the bill goes back to Congress for a new vote

   C. the bill does not become a law

   D. the bill becomes a law

2. What check on executive power is shown in the law-making process?

   A. the impeachment power of Congress

   B. the judicial review power of the Supreme Court

   C. the veto power of the president

   D. the presidential veto override power of Congress

3. What is the purpose of a Congressional conference committee?

   A. to propose new bills

   B. to amend bills

   C. to study proposed bills

   D. to vote on bills

4. Why do you think Congressional overrides of vetoes are so rare?

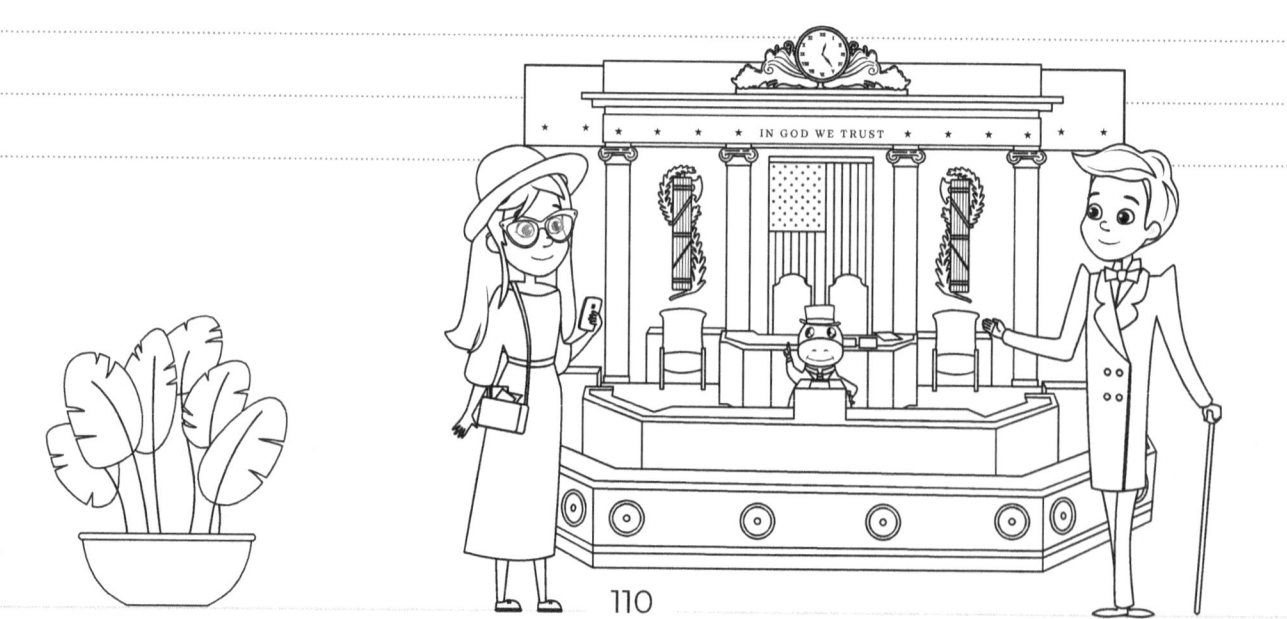

Directions: Read the text below. Then answer the questions that follow.

Last week, you learned that the first ten amendments to the Constitution are called the **Bill of Rights** and that they were added to the Constitution because of concerns by Anti-Federalists. The Bill of Rights protects some of your most important liberties.

Amendment	What it does
First	Protects your **freedom of speech; freedom of the press**; and **freedom of religion**. It also prevents government from backing one religion over another. The amendment also gives people to the **right to assemble** to protest or **petition** (formally ask) the government to address an issue.
Second	Protects the **right to bear arms**.
Third	Stops the government from using people's home to **house armed forces**; this was a problem in the colonial era.
Fourth	Protects your person and property by not allowing **unreasonable search and seizure** by the government.
Fifth	Serious crimes must be heard by a **grand jury**. A person **cannot be put on trial for the same crime twice**. Property cannot be taken away by the government without **just compensation**. People cannot be put in prison without **due process of law** such as a jury trial. People have the right not to **self-incriminate** themselves.
Sixth	People have the right to a **speedy trial by an impartial (fair) jury**.
Seventh	A jury trial is required in federal civil cases.
Eighth	Government is not allowed to inflict excessive bail or carry out **cruel and unusual punishment.**
Ninth	People have **other rights** even if they are not spelled out in the Constitution.
Tenth	The federal government only has the rights granted to them by the Constitution. All other rights go to the states or the people.

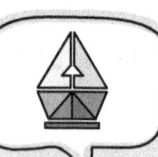
1. Which of the following issues would be covered under the First Amendment?

   A. a law restricting the use of firearms in public areas

   B. a debate over capital punishment

   C. a person who was put in prison without a trial

   D. an online blog posting an article critical of a senator

2. The Tenth Amendment protects which rights?

   A. the rights of states such as New York

   B. the rights of people accused of crimes

   C. the rights of people to practice religion

   D. the rights of a person to carry a weapon

3. A person is accused of a crime and is put on trial. The person then refuses to testify, citing Fifth Amendment rights since that person does not want to tell a lie while on trial. What right is that person exercising?

....

....

....

4. How does the Bill of Rights help build a stronger society?

....

....

....

Directions: Read the text below. Then answer the questions that follow.

The Bill of Rights is very important to all of us as citizens. Think about some of your daily activities.

1. What would be an example in your daily life of you exercising a First Amendment right?

2. Of the rights and protections in the Bill of Rights, what are the most important three rights to you? Why?

3. Fill out the chart below by writing the amendment number and the right that protects citizens in each scenario.

Police come to Billy's home, force open the door, and then take his computer saying that it is for evidence.	Amendment #............. Right ....
A certain church is banned from holding services because they are having a disagreement with the local mayor.	Amendment #............. Right ....
A student is suspended from school for voicing an unpopular opinion about the government.	Amendment #............. Right ....
A citizen knows he is guilty of a crime but will not give testimony against himself in court.	Amendment #............. Right ....
A group of people did not like a new law and marched down a main street to make their views known.	Amendment #............. Right ....

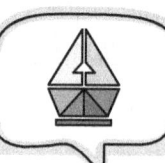
Directions: Read the text below. Then answer the questions that follow.

This week you learned about the U.S. Constitution and how it applies to you. You also learned about the Bill of Rights and how it protects some of your most important freedoms.

1. Based on the structure of government and the separation of powers, do you think any one branch of government is stronger than the others? Why or why not?

2. Summarize the process for how a bill becomes a law.

3. Consider what you have learned last week about the ratification of the Constitution and the Anti-federalists. Why is the Tenth Amendment important? Why is the entire Bill of Rights important in this context?

History

Testing the Constitution

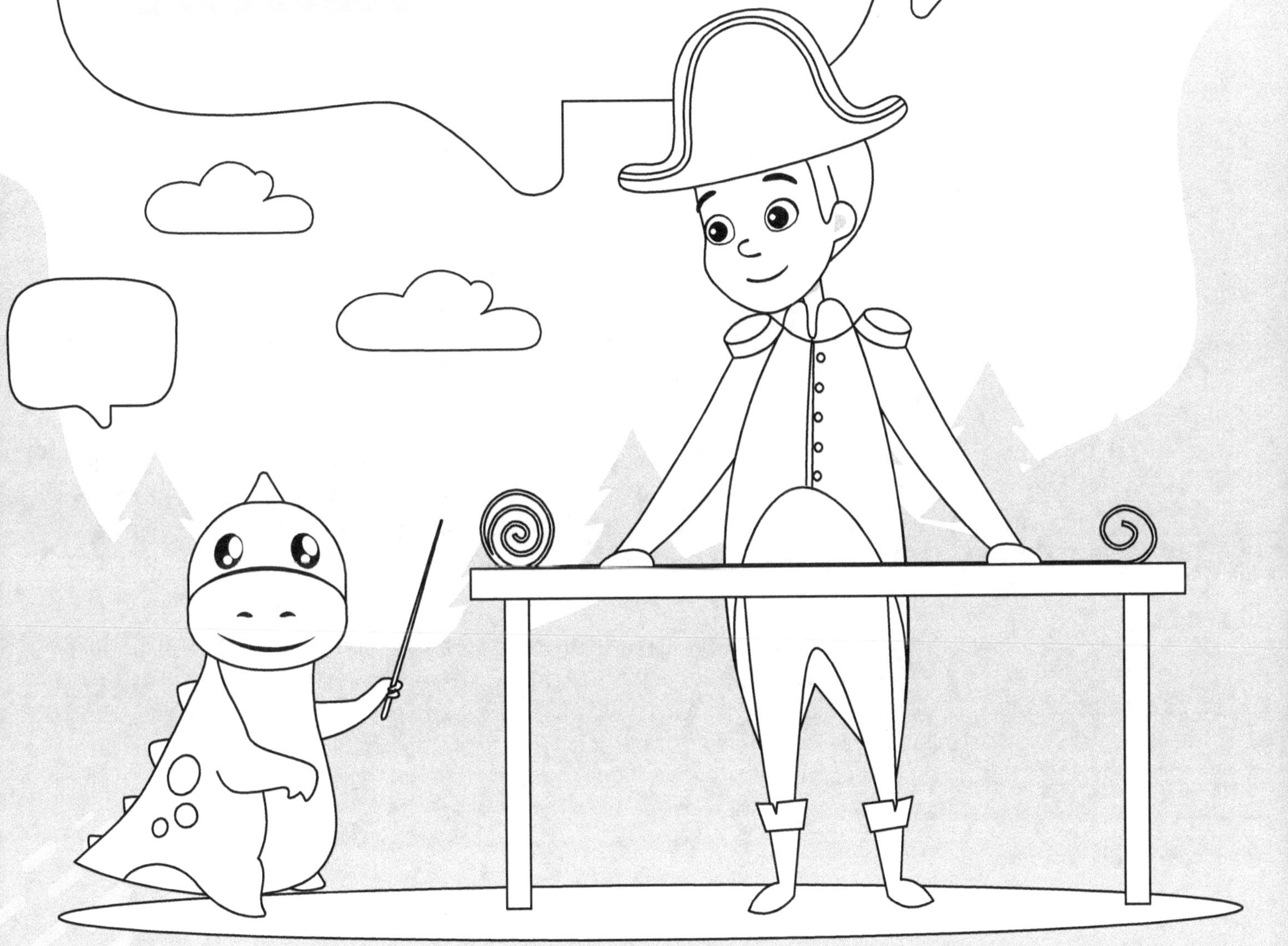

This week, you will learn about the first decades after the adoption of the U.S. Constitution and how it underwent different tests.

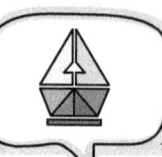
Directions: Read the text below. Then answer the questions that follow.

In the first decades after the adoption of the Constitution, the country underwent numerous challenges which tested the strength of the new government. The first major test had to do with resolving some of the problems from the Revolutionary War period. The individual states as well as the national government were still in debt. To solve this, President George Washington's Secretary of the Treasury, **Alexander Hamilton**, proposed new taxes as well as a plan for improving the economy. While the plan passed Congress, it upset some, because the plan included the creation of a national bank. Opponents complained that the power of the federal government to create a bank was not an **enumerated power**, or a power clearly listed in the Constitution. Hamilton, however, argued that the Constitution did state that the government could make "all laws which are necessary and proper." These, he argued, are **implied powers**, or powers that are not spelled out clearly in the Constitution, but are still allowed.

Hamilton, who believed in a strong central government, became one of the leaders of the **Federalist Party**. He came into conflict with Washington's Secretary of State, Thomas Jefferson. **Thomas Jefferson** and James Madison were leaders of what became known as **Democratic-Republican Party**, and argued that states should have more power than the federal government.

Washington wasn't a member of any political party, as he believed political parties hurt the country. Washington was important in setting **precedents** for the presidency, including only serving for two terms. When Washington stepped down in 1796, his vice-president **John Adams**, a Federalist, ran against Jefferson. Adams won by a narrow margin and became president.

The Adams Administration argued with Jefferson and the Democratic-Republicans. Jefferson and Adams ran against each other again in the election of 1800 in a very hard campaign. Jefferson won, and Adams stepped down from the presidency. This event was important since it was the first peaceful transfer of power from one political party to the other in American history.

1. Who was a leader of the Federalist Party?

   A. George Washington

   B. Thomas Jefferson

   C. Alexander Hamilton

   D. James Madison

2. Why did some people object to Hamilton's plan for a national bank?

   A. They argued that it would strengthen the powers of the states too much.

   B. They argued that it would weaken the powers of the federal government.

   C. They argued that it was only an enumerated power of the federal government.

   D. They argued that it wasn't a power given to the federal government.

3. Why was the election of 1800 important?

   A. It was the first transfer of power between political parties in American history.

   B. It brought the Federalist party into power for the first time.

   C. It demonstrated the new federal government's authority for the first time.

   D. It was the first use of implied powers by the Democratic-Republicans.

4. What are implied powers?

   A. powers in the Constitution over monetary matters

   B. powers in the Constitution given to the states

   C. powers in the Constitution that are clearly delegated

   D. powers in the Constitution that are not spelled out

Jefferson

Adams

Directions: Read the text below. Then answer the questions that follow.

Thomas Jefferson became the third president of the United States. The country continued to develop and test its new Constitution. The next challenge concerned court appointments. After John Adams lost the re-election of 1800, he appointed Federalist judges before leaving office in order to maintain some power in the judicial branch of government. One of the judges, William Marbury, was appointed but did not receive an official commission before the transfer of power from Adams to Jefferson. After Jefferson came into office, he ordered that the commission not be delivered. Marbury then sued Jefferson's Secretary of State, James Madison. The case of *Marbury v. Madison* went to the Supreme Court. The Supreme Court was led by Chief Justice **John Marshall**. Marshall ruled that Jefferson was wrong to order Madison not to give the commission, but that the part of the law allowing Marbury to be a judge was **unconstitutional** - that is, it went against the Constitution and was therefore illegal. This gave Jefferson a win, but it was also the first time that the Supreme Court used the power of **judicial review**, which is the power of the court to determine if a law is constitutional or not. As a result, the case of *Marbury v. Madison* set a legal **precedent** that the Supreme Court could declare laws unconstitutional. This is one way that the judicial branch can check the power of the other branches of government.

1. Who made the ruling in *Marbury v. Madison?*

   A. John Marshall

   B. Thomas Jefferson

   C. William Marbury

   D. James Madison

2. What was the issue of the case in *Marbury v. Madison?*

   A. judicial review

   B. court appointments

   C. presidential power

   D. legislative power

3. What is judicial review?

    A. the power of the Supreme Court to determine if a law is unconstitutional

    B. the power of the Supreme Court to create laws that follow the Constitution

    C. the power of the Supreme Court to appoint federal judges

    D. the power of the Supreme Court to check the executive branch

4. What was the long term importance of *Marbury v. Madison*?

    A. Presidents could appoint federal judges

    B. The Supreme Court could declare laws unconstitutional

    C. The Federalists controlled the judiciary

    D. The Executive branch was stronger than the judicial.

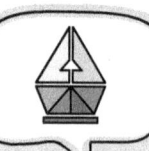
Directions: Read the text below. Then answer the questions that follow.

Jefferson, as you have learned, supported a limited federal government. However, in 1803 he received an offer from Napoleon Bonaparte, the emperor of France, to sell the Louisiana Territory to the United States. Jefferson questioned whether he had the authority to buy the land, but he did it anyway since the land would likely become very valuable. The territory included the important port of New Orleans. The United States bought the Louisiana Territory for $15 million, which amounted to about four cents per acre. **The Louisiana Purchase** nearly doubled the size of the United States at that time.

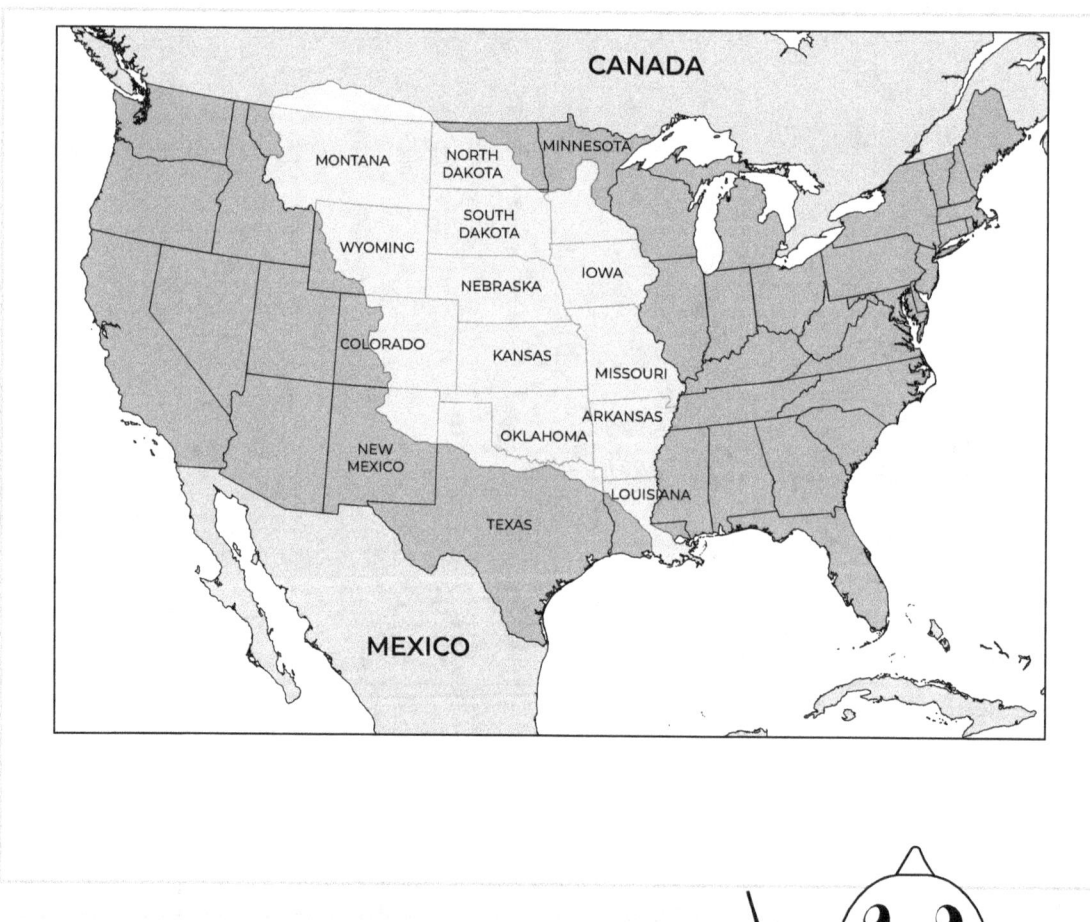

1. What did the Louisiana Purchase do?

   A. regulate trade to New Orleans

   B. establish new states like Kansas

   C. increase French territory

   D. double the size of the United States

2. What did Jefferson question about the Louisiana Purchase?

    A. whether he had the right to do it

    B. whether the country could afford it

    C. whether it would start a war

    D. whether it was worth doing

3. What current states have territory that was part of the Louisiana Purchase?

_____

_____

_____

4. Who sold Louisiana to the United States?

_____

_____

_____

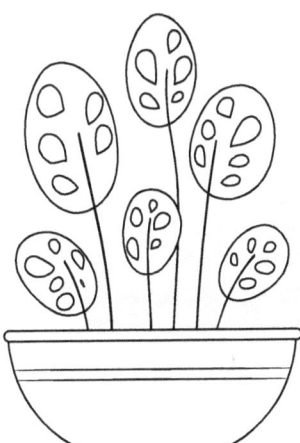

Directions: Read the text below. Then answer the questions that follow.

Two concepts you learned about this week were **enumerated powers** and **implied powers**. To review, enumerated powers are powers granted to the government that are spelled out clearly in the Constitution, while implied powers are not spelled out clearly.

1. When purchasing the Louisiana Territory, was Jefferson using enumerated or implied powers?

2. Thomas Jefferson was a Democratic-Republican who supported states rights over a strong federal government. Do you think this influenced his decision to purchase the Louisiana Territory? Why or why not?

3. Do you think it is better to have powers enumerated or implied? What are the advantages and disadvantages?

Directions: Read the text below. Then answer the questions that follow.

This week you learned about the early decades after the establishment of the Constitution and some of the important events that occurred during this time that tested and expanded the nation.

1. How did the arguments over the Constitution continue into the early years of the republic?

....

....

....

....

2. Why is *Marbury v. Madison* important in terms of constitutional concepts such as checks and balances?

....

....

....

....

3. What do you think the perspective of Native Americans was regarding the Louisiana Purchase?

....

....

....

....

4. Why was George Washington important as the country's first president?

....

....

....

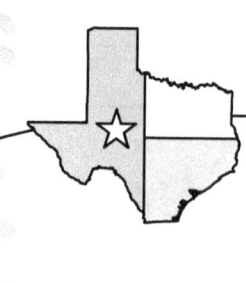

Geography
Westward Expansion

U.S. TERRITORIAL ACQUISITIONS

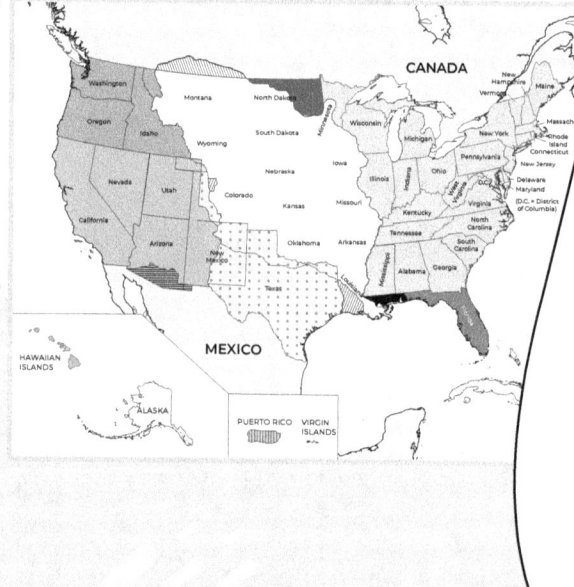

This week, you will learn about how the United States expanded West in the first decades of the 19th century and how that led to conflict with Native Americans.

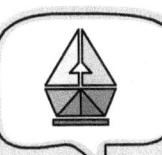
Directions: Read the text below. Then answer the questions that follow.

"

After the Louisiana Purchase, the United States started to look westward. Americans came to believe that their country was meant to expand across the continent. This belief was called **manifest destiny.**

Opportunity to expand came after the **War of 1812**. This war, which was a second conflict between the United States and Britain, ended in a draw. However, the war expanded America's boundaries, and it also resulted in the United States taking land from the many Native American tribes who sided with the British, such as the Creek and Cherokee.

The United States also acquired Florida from Spain in 1819. Afterwards, the United States tried to purchase Texas from Mexico, but Mexico refused. Meanwhile, Americans were settling in Texas. In 1836, Americans in Texas declared independence from Mexico. Texans then overwhelmingly pushed for **annexation** by the United States. In 1845, Texas officially became a state. The annexation outraged Mexico and led to a war between the two countries from 1846 to 1848. This was called the **Mexican-American War**. The United States won and as a result, Mexico **ceded**, or gave up lands, including California and much of the American southwest in what is now called the **Mexican Cession**.

By 1848, the United States had achieved manifest destiny. However, there were clouds on the horizon. Controversy continued to erupt as to whether these new lands would allow or forbid slavery. This issue would lead to the American Civil War.

"

1. What is manifest destiny?

   A. the belief that the United States should conquer Native Americans

   B. the belief that the United States should control the continent

   C. the belief that the United States should spread democracy

   D. the belief that the United States should annex Texas

2. What was a result of the War of 1812?

    A. the Louisiana purchase   **C.** the annexation of Texas

    B. new American boundaries   **D.** the Mexican cession

3. Who pushed for the annexation of Texas by the United States?

    A. the Mexican government   **C.** Americans in Texas

    B. Native Americans   **D.** the British government

4. What was an area acquired by the Mexican Cession?

    A. Ohio

    B. Florida

    C. California

    D. Texas

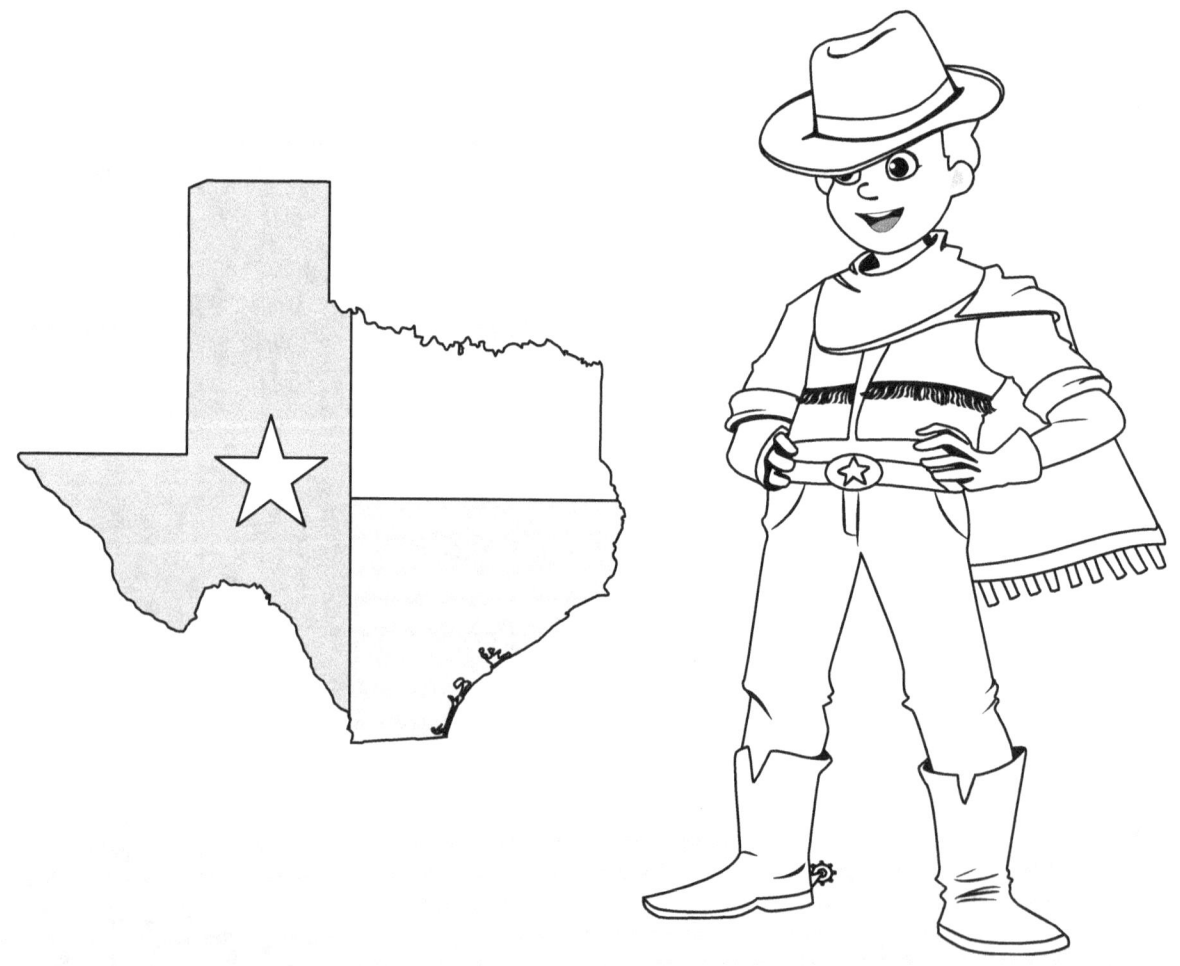

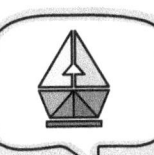
Directions: Read the text below. Then answer the questions that follow.

"

This map explores the ways in which the United States expanded. Maps of the United States usually contain the **continental** United States, which are the parts of the country that are contiguous, or connected to one another. The **contiguous** United States does not include Alaska, Hawaii, Puerto Rico, or the Virgin Islands. In this map, Alaska, Hawaii, Puerto Rico, and the Virgin Islands are added to the map in the lower left corner.

U.S. TERRITORIAL ACQUISITIONS

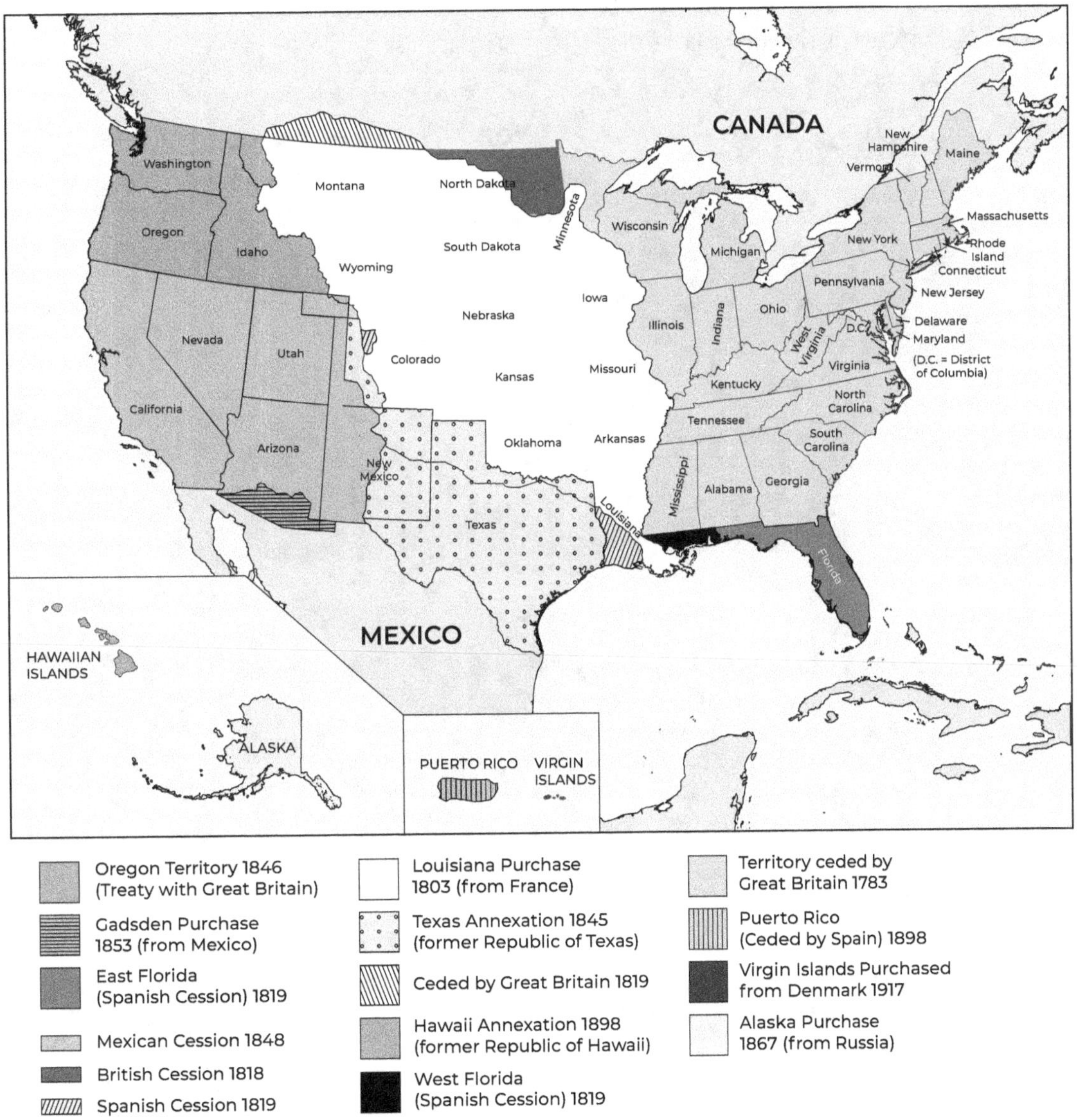

Legend:

- Oregon Territory 1846 (Treaty with Great Britain)
- Gadsden Purchase 1853 (from Mexico)
- East Florida (Spanish Cession) 1819
- Mexican Cession 1848
- British Cession 1818
- Spanish Cession 1819
- Louisiana Purchase 1803 (from France)
- Texas Annexation 1845 (former Republic of Texas)
- Ceded by Great Britain 1819
- Hawaii Annexation 1898 (former Republic of Hawaii)
- West Florida (Spanish Cession) 1819
- Territory ceded by Great Britain 1783
- Puerto Rico (Ceded by Spain) 1898
- Virgin Islands Purchased from Denmark 1917
- Alaska Purchase 1867 (from Russia)

"

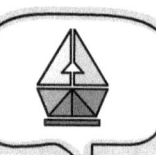
1. According to the map, which piece of territory was acquired last by the United States in the continental United States?

    A. Northwest Minnesota

    B. Florida

    C. Missouri

    D. Southern Arizona

2. In what year did the United States acquire the territory that includes Idaho?

    A. 1803   **B.** 1846   **C.** 1867   **D.** 1819

3. Use the chart and place American territorial acquisitions listed below in the correct chronological order, labeling the year for each:

Territory	Year it was acquired by the United States

Mexican Cession, Gadsden Purchase, Louisiana Purchase, East Florida, Oregon Territory, Texas Annexation

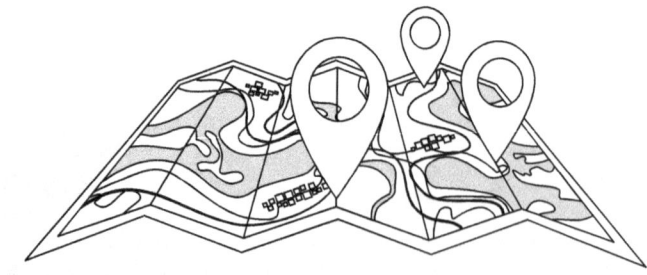

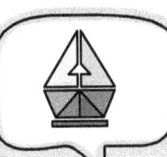
Directions: Read the text below. Then answer the questions that follow.

"The westward expansion of the United States brought numerous settlers looking to start new lives on land they could call their own. However, they came into immediate conflict with Native American tribes living in those lands.

During the presidency of **Andrew Jackson**, the push to open lands to American settlement grew. In 1830, Congress passed the **Indian Removal Act** which forced Native Americans who lived east of the Mississippi to relocate west. This act impacted Native Americans in the southeast such as the Creek, Cherokee, Chickasaw, and Chocktaw. Most tribes had no choice but to follow the order, since the United States military was much more powerful, but the Cherokee, who lived in Georgia, did not. They brought their case before the Supreme Court, but the court refused to hear the case, saying the Cherokee did not have the standing, or the right, to sue, since they were not considered citizens. Eventually, Jackson's successor, **Martin Van Buren** sent the army to remove the Cherokee in 1838 and force them to relocate to what is now Oklahoma. During the march, about 4,000 Cherokee people died of disease, starvation, and exposure. This journey has been named the **Trail of Tears**."

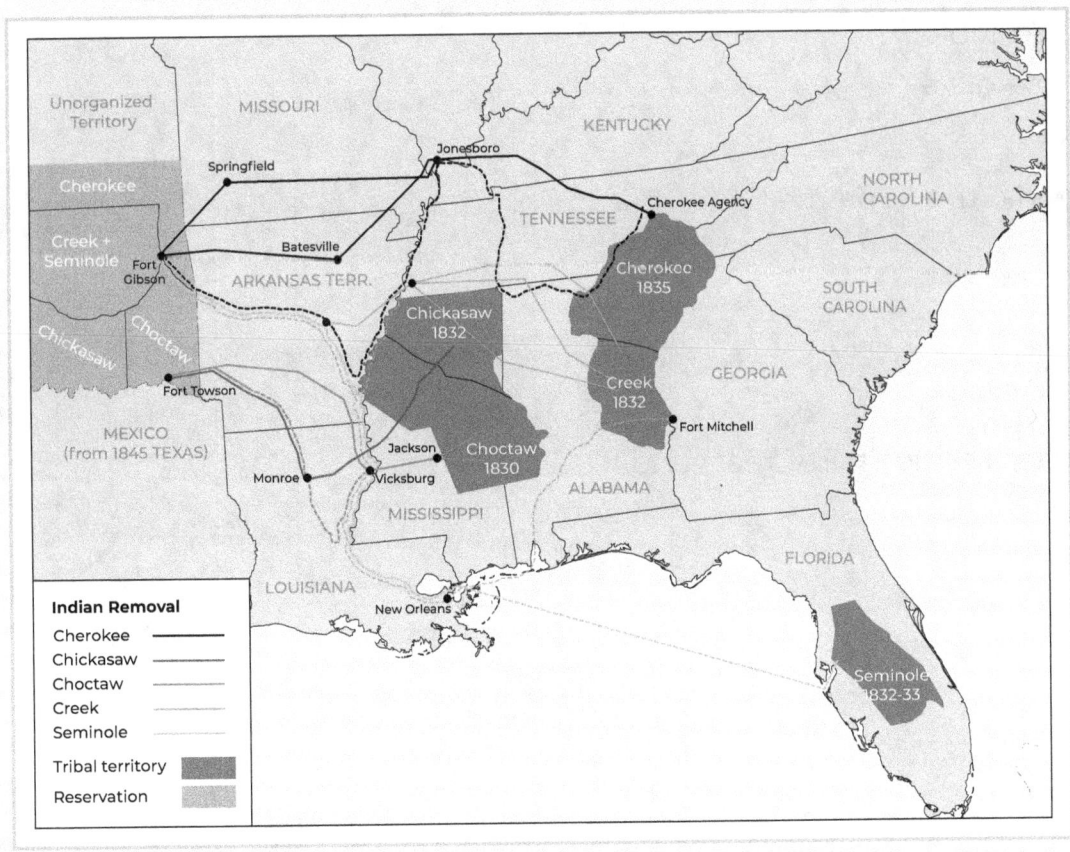

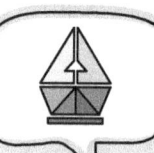
"

Another group that resisted removal were the Seminole in Florida. Between 1835 and 1842 the Seminole waged a guerilla war against the United States. While there were only a few thousand Seminole warriors against some 30,000 American troops, they fought for years before they finally surrendered. About 2,000 Americans were killed in the conflict.

"

1. The Indian Removal Act of 1830

   A. declared war of Native Americans east of the Mississippi.
   B. forced Native Americans to relocate west of the Mississippi.
   C. reaffirmed Native American rights as sovereign nations.
   D. let individual states decide how to treat Native Americans.

2. Which Native American group resisted American efforts to remove them through warfare?

   A. Choctaw
   B. Seminole
   C. Cherokee
   D. Creek

3. How did the Supreme Court rule against the Cherokee?

   ....

   ....

   ....

4. Where did the Trail of Tears end? ....

Directions: Read the text below. Then answer the questions that follow.

The following passages are excerpts from letters written by President Andrew Jackson and Cherokee leader John Ross.

From Andrew Jackson to the Cherokee, 1835:

"You are now placed in the midst of a white population. Your peculiar customs.... have been abrogated [done away with] by the great political community among which you live.... You are liable to prosecutions for offences, and to civil actions for a breach of any of your contracts.-Most of your people are uneducated, and are liable to be brought into collision at all times with their white neighbors. Your young men are acquiring habits of intoxication. With strong passions, and without those habits of restraint, which our laws... render necessary, they are frequently driven to excesses which must eventually terminate in their ruin."

From John Ross to Andrew Jackson, 1836:

"...we are despoiled [robbed] of our private possessions.... We are stripped of every attribute of freedom.... Our property may be plundered before our eyes; violence may be committed on our persons; even our lives may be taken away, and there is none to regard our complaints. We are denationalized; we are disfranchised. We are deprived of membership in the human family! We have neither land nor home, nor resting place that can be called our own.... We are overwhelmed! Our hearts are sickened, our utterance is paralized, when we reflect on the condition in which we are placed, by the audacious practices of unprincipled men...."

1. What do you think is Andrew Jackson's purpose in writing the letter to the Cherokee?

....

....

....

2. What is the key theme or idea behind Ross's letter?

....

....

....

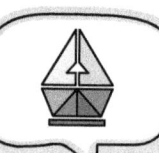
3. What is Andrew Jackson warning to the Cherokee in his letter?

....

....

....

4. What does Jackson say is happening to the Cherokee? What is the flaw in this argument?

....

....

....

5. What letter are you more sympathetic with? Why?

....

....

....

Directions: Answer the questions below.

This week you learned about the territorial expansion of the United States westward and its impact on Native Americans.

1. What were the costs of manifest destiny?

_____

_____

_____

_____

2. What seems to be the primary driver for American expansion westward?

_____

_____

_____

_____

3. Do you think westward expansion made conflict with Native Americans inevitable? Why or why not?

_____

_____

_____

_____

4. Without westward expansion, how would have the United States been different geographically and economically?

_____

_____

_____

Economics

The Early Industrialization of America

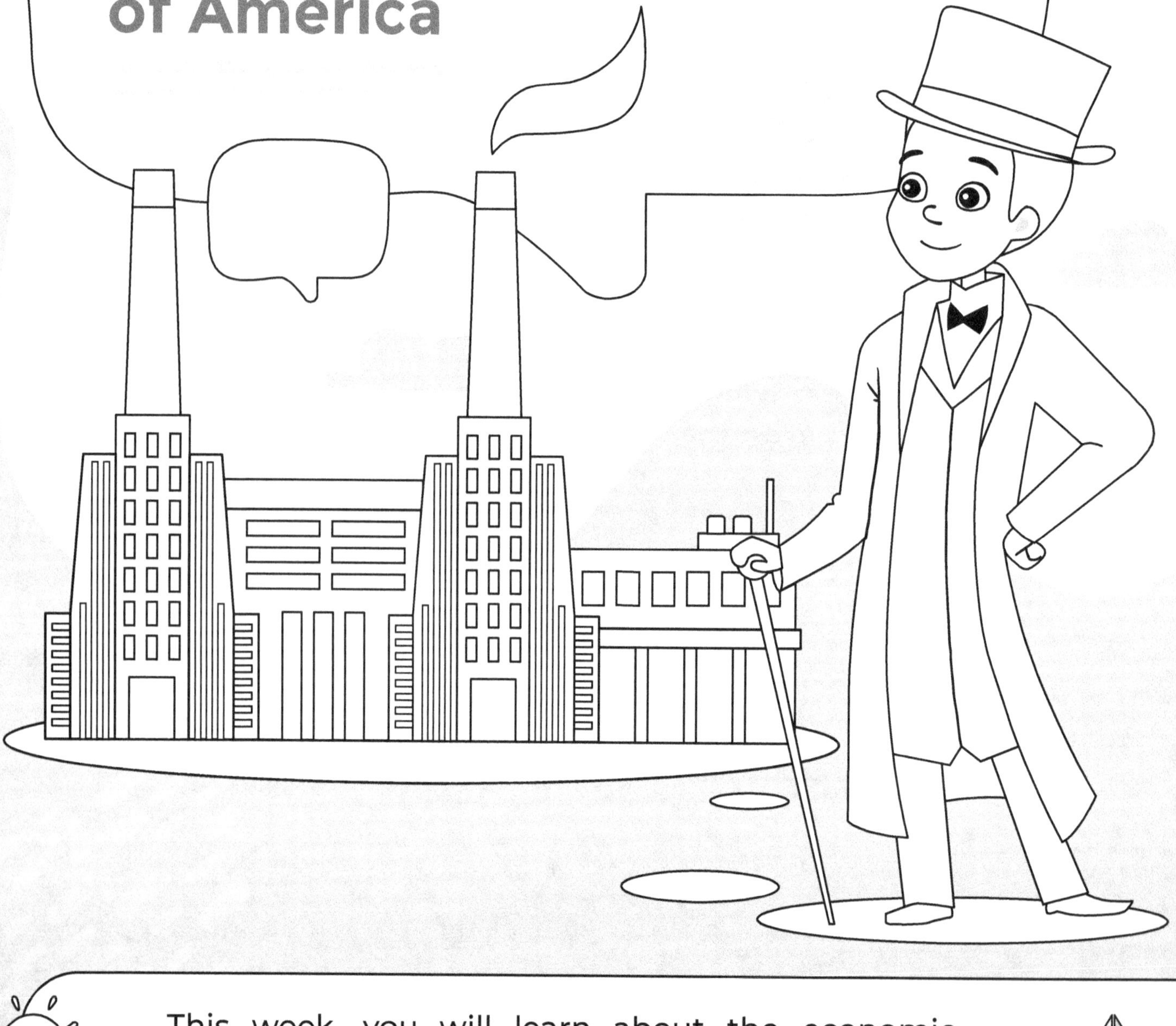

This week, you will learn about the economic development and growth of the United States including its industrialization.

ARGOPREP

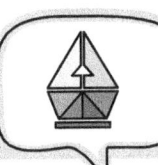
Directions: Read the text below. Then answer the questions that follow.

As you learned last week, the United States expanded westward in the first half of the 19th century. This expansion occurred simultaneously with the economic development of the United States. One of the first major steps in this development was the building of the nation's transportation infrastructure. One of the first people to conceive of this idea was Senator **Henry Clay**, who proposed an **American System** in which the federal government would help develop the country's economy.

The first major east-west highway built by the federal government was the **National Road**, also called the Cumberland Road. It was built between 1811 and 1818. This road stretched from Cumberland, Maryland, to Wheeling, Virginia (now West Virginia) and was used by thousands of settlers heading west. The road would continue to extend west as it developed over the years. Other states built roads as well; New York built 4,000 miles of roads. The country was becoming more connected.

Another improvement in transportation was the construction of the **Erie Canal**, which was largely backed by New York's governor, **DeWitt Clinton**. Finished in 1825, the canal connected the Hudson River to the Great Lakes. The connection allowed goods from the West to be shipped to the East where they would eventually reach New York City and beyond. The Erie Canal helped to make New York City the country's biggest and most important seaport. These water routes became even more important after the development of the **steamboat**. Powered by a steam engine instead of a sail, it could travel against wind and current. In 1807, **Robert Fulton** and **Robert R. Livingston** demonstrated the potential of the steam engine by sailing Clermont (the first steamboat in public service) up the Hudson River from New York to reach Albany in 32 hours.

Yet the greatest impact on the transportation network was the **railroad**. Starting in 1830 the country started to lay down thousands of miles of track. By 1861, there were over 30,000 miles of railroad. Transportation improvements developed the American economy by allowing people and goods to travel faster and farther than ever before.

1. What is the importance of the National Road?

   A. It was a major route for western settlement.

   B. It connected the Hudson River to the Great Lakes.

   C. It made travel against wind and current possible.

   D. It connected the South to the North.

2. What did the Erie Canal connect?

   A. Wheeling, Virginia to New York City

   B. Albany, New York to New York City

   C. Cumberland, Maryland to Wheeling, Virginia

   D. New York City to the Great Lakes

3. Who proposed the American System?

   A. Henry Clay

   B. DeWitt Clinton

   C. Robert Fulton

   D. Robert R. Livingston

4. The *Clermont* is most associated with

   A. the growth of canals.

   B. the building of railroads.

   C. the development of the steamboat.

   D. the construction of the Cumberland Road.

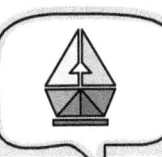
Directions: Read the text below. Then answer the questions that follow.

"

The growth of America's transportation network accelerated its **industrialization**. Industrialization is the transition from hand-made goods to factory-made goods. The rapid transition to industrial production is called the **Industrial Revolution**. The Industrial Revolution occurred first in Britain in the 18th century, where goods once made by skilled workers in shops or in homes were replaced by workers making those same goods in factories.

The first factory in the United States is credited to **Samuel Slater** who borrowed heavily from British technology and helped start up a factory in Rhode Island in 1793. By the early 19th century, these ideas of production spread mainly in the Northeast because it had ample rivers and streams that could power water mills. In 1814, **Francis C. Lowell** opened a series of textile mills in Massachusetts. Lowell typically hired women to work in the factories since he could pay them lower wages. In the following decades, industrialization spread to all sorts of products. This process was also accelerated by new inventions.

Factory owners adopted the use of **interchangeable parts**. Interchangeable parts are simply identical parts that can be assembled easily. Before interchangeable parts, pieces were made by hand, which meant that the parts in one item wouldn't work in another. The inventor **Eli Whitney** popularized this process, and it greatly sped up production.

Another important development was the invention of the telegraph by **Samuel Morse** in the 1830s. This invention allowed for messages to be sent in electrical code over wire. What this meant was that news and information, which traveled slowly before, could now be transmitted instantaneously. Businesses and the government immediately saw its value. In 1858, a transatlantic telegraph cable connected Europe and the United States for the first time. By 1860 over 50,000 miles of telegraph connected the country.

"

1. _____ was known as an early pioneer in opening textile mills in Massachusetts.

   A. Samuel Morse
   B. Francis C. Lowell
   C. Samuel Slater
   D. Eli Whitney

2. The invention of the telegraph revolutionized

    A. agriculture.

    B. manufacturing.

    C. transportation.

    D. communication.

3. What is industrialization?

    A. the transition from hand-made goods to mass manufacture of goods by machine

    B. the capability of communicating instantly

    C. the change of labor from unskilled to skilled

    D. the use of unique parts to make hand-crafted tools

4. How did the Industrial Revolution impact labor?

    A. More people worked in factories.

    B. More people handmade their goods.

    C. More people worked in agriculture.

    D. More people became homebound.

Directions: Read the text below. Then answer the questions that follow.

The Industrial Revolution created new jobs in the United States. These jobs were located primarily in urban areas. This led to the growth in cities, particularly in the northern parts of the country where industrialization took root. New York City took the lead as the largest city in the country, becoming its manufacturing and financial center. In 1800, the population of the city was about 60,000. By 1860, the population had grown to over one million people. Urban growth created problems such as unsanitary conditions, disease, and increased crime. Also, there was an ever increasing danger of fire as cities grew.

The population of cities grew due to large numbers of people moving from rural to urban areas, but also to increased immigration to the United States. One of the largest sources of immigrants during this time was Ireland. Starting in 1845, a blight ruined Ireland's potato crops, which was the primary source of food for the people. The resulting famine drove people to leave their country. Between 1847 and 1854, 1.25 million Irish immigrants moved to the United States. These immigrants often took low paying jobs in the new factories. Irish were often discriminated against for being foreign-born and for practicing Catholicism. Many lived in poverty. By far, they were the largest immigrant group of the period.

As the country expanded economically and demographically, it also became economically unstable. With little regulation over the economy, the country went through intense periods of economic booms and busts. All of these factors created a country that was becoming heavily divided between rich and poor and also by geographic sections. Eventually, it was these sectional differences that would lead to conflict.

1. What was an effect of industrialization?

    A. decrease in immigration

    B. increase in urban growth

    C. decrease in number of jobs

    D. increase in agricultural production

2. Why did the risk of fires increase in cities during the early 19th century?

    A. because of increased immigration

    B. because of the growth of factories

    C. because of a rise in crime

    D. because of rapid population growth

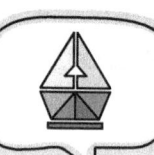
3. Explain how industrialization and immigration are linked.

....

....

....

....

4. What challenges did Irish immigrants face?

....

....

....

....

....

Directions: Read the text below. Then answer the questions that follow.

Industrialization changed the United States economically and socially. Some scholars argue that the United States is currently undergoing an Information Revolution based on computer technology.

1. What type of technology revolutionized communication in the early Industrial Revolution?

2. What type of technologies do you use to communicate today?

3. Has the way in which goods and people travel changed much since the Industrial Revolution? Explain the differences.

4. How have computers changed people's jobs? How have they harmed other kinds of jobs?

Directions: Read the text below. Then answer the questions that follow.

This week you learned about economic and social changes in the early United States.

1. Describe three to four ways industrialization changed the United States.

....

....

....

....

2. Elaborate on how transportation and industrialization are linked.

....

....

....

....

3. How did the Erie Canal help New York become America's largest city?

....

....

....

....

4. How were interchangeable parts critical for industrialization?

....

....

....

....

....

....

WEEK 15

Economics

Slavery in America

This week, you will learn about the reasons for the growth of slavery in the United States and how enslaved people fought against that system.

ARGOPREP

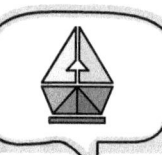
Directions: Read the text below. Then answer the questions that follow.

As you learned last week, the North went through an industrial revolution during the 19th century. The South developed too, but its economy was largely dependent on the system of slavery. New inventions in the 19th century, such as the invention of the **cotton gin** by Eli Whitney, helped make plantation owners even more money, and increased their desire for even more free labor. In 1793, Whitney noticed that it often took an entire day to separate a pound of usable cotton from its seeds. His invention combed out the seeds quickly and efficiently. Because Whitney's invention occurred while there was a boom in industrialized textile mills in Europe, demand for cotton was high. Very quickly, the cotton gin was adopted and cotton became so dominant as a commodity in the South that the saying "Cotton is King" became commonplace. The region remained agricultural with only a few major cities: New Orleans, Charleston, and Baltimore.

Growing and harvesting cotton was labor intensive. Thus, with the rise of demand for cotton came a sharp increase in demand for labor. As cotton production increased, so too did the number of enslaved persons in the South.

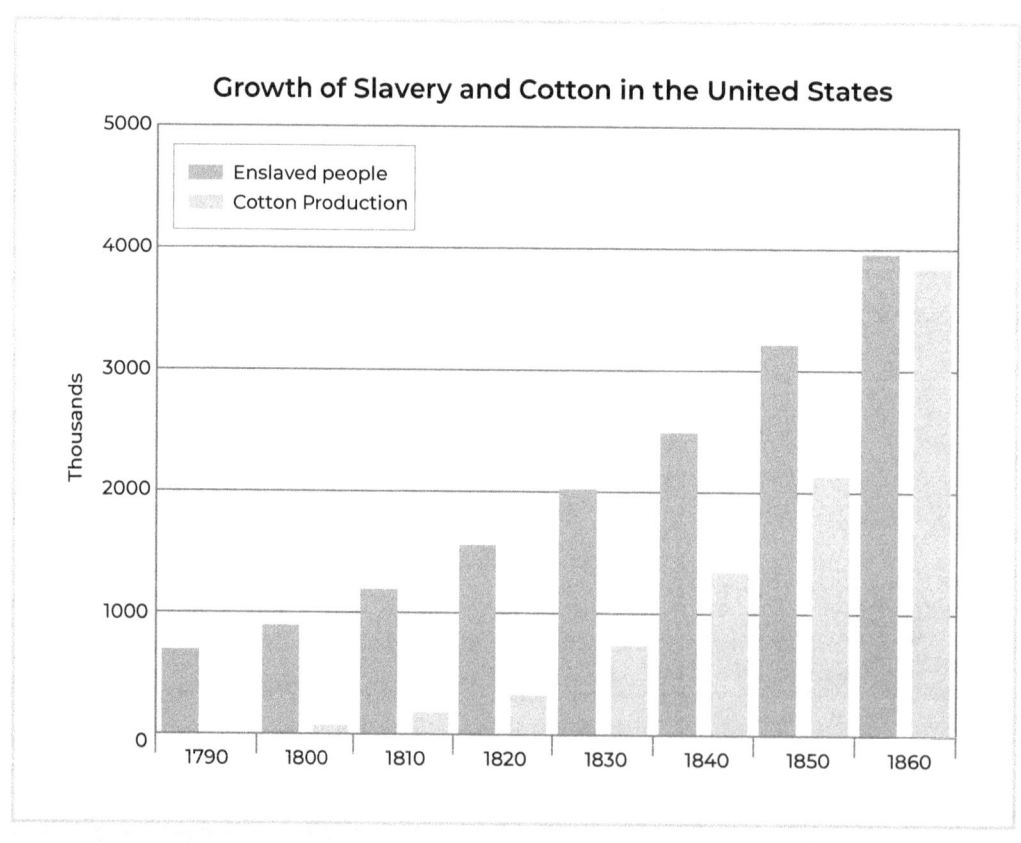

1. The cotton gin was an invention that

    A. sped up the harvesting of cotton.

    B. sped up the processing of cotton.

    C. sped up the planting of cotton.

    D. sped up the sale of cotton.

2. What drove the demand for cotton?

    A. the increase of enslaved persons

    B. the rise of southern cities

    C. the growth of textile mills

    D. the invention of the cotton gin

3. What relationship does the chart in this section describe?

    A. the relationship between the growth of cotton production and the growth of slavery

    B. the relationship between the increase in cotton production and the decline in slavery

    C. the relationship between the decline in cotton production and the growth of slavery

    D. the relationship between the decline in cotton production and the decline in slavery

4. According to the chart, what year had the highest population of enslaved people living in the United States?

    A. 1860

    B. 1790

    C. 1820

    D. 1850

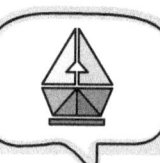
Directions: Read the text below. Then answer the questions that follow.

Southern society was impacted by its slavery-based economic system. In the South, there was a strong social **hierarchy**. At the very top of the hierarchy were elite **planters** who owned the largest plantations and held the most enslaved people -- 20 or more slaves. The elite planters amounted to some 38,000 families across all slave states. This constituted less than one percent of the entire white southern population, yet this group dominated the region's economy and politics.

Under the elite planters were a small group of professionals such as lawyers, doctors, merchants, and others who also invested in larger plantations or owned their own farms. This group tended to live in the cities. The vast majority of whites in the South were yeoman farmers who owned modest sized farms. The lowest rungs of white society were the rural poor who lived often on barren lands and barely grew enough food to feed themselves. At the very bottom of the social hierarchy were the enslaved African Americans, who by 1850 numbered 3.6 million people, accounting for over one-third of the entire population of the South. While not all white people in the South (nearly 65%) owned enslaved people, most whites were invested in a social and economic system that depended on and promoted slavery.

Most enslaved people worked in agriculture in the South's rural areas, but a large number also worked in southern cities in a variety of industries and as domestic servants or tradesmen. Regardless of where enslaved African Americans worked, they were subject to abuse and dehumanization. This treatment led enslaved people to find ways to seek freedom.

1. Where did most enslaved people work?

   A. small farms

   B. plantations

   C. factories

   D. urban homes

2. Which social class was at the top of the South's social hierarchy?

   A. enslaved people

   B. yeoman farmers

   C. planters

   D. professionals

3. Which of the following statements is true?

    A. Enslaved people made up the majority of the population in the South.

    B. Professional classes in southern cities controlled the large plantations.

    C. Yeomen lived in cities and invested in plantations.

    D. Plantation owners dominated the economy and politics of the South.

4. Why did most Southerners support slavery?

....

....

....

....

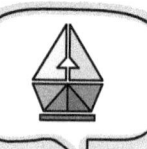
Directions: Read the text below. Then answer the questions that follow.

Millions of African Americans were enslaved in America during the first half of the 19th century. Some enslaved people resisted oppression. Usually, this entailed slowing down work, breaking tools, destroying property, or running away. Occasionally, enslaved people would kill their owners. In each instance, enslaved people risked public beating, mutilation, or execution. However, there were also instances of planned revolt. The timeline below shows some of the major revolts against slavery during the first half of the 19th century.

Year	Details	Result
1800	The enslaved **Gabriel Prosser** organized an uprising where resisters crafted their own weapons. They planned to capture Richmond, Virginia and kill whites who supported slavery.	The plot was exposed and Governor James Monroe activated the state militia. Prosser and others were captured, tried, and executed.
1811	**Charles Deslondes**, an enslaved person, led a revolt in Louisiana, gathering the force of around 500 enslaved people. They burned plantations and other property.	Plantation owners summoned the militia and Charles Deslondes was killed in the fighting. Others were executed after the fact.
1816	In this revolt, 300 enslaved people and 20 Native American allies took and held Fort Blount in Florida.	After holding the fort for several days, American soldiers attacked and retook the fort, ending the revolt.
1822	**Denmark Vessey**, a free African American in Charleston, South Carolina, was accused of planning an armed revolt with the goal of freeing enslaved people.	Vessey was arrested, tried, and hanged. It is debated if Vessey actually plotted a revolt.

Year	Details	Result
1831	**Nat Turner**, who was born into slavery, led a revolt in Virginia leading to the deaths of about 50 white men, women and children. Turner believed that he was ordained by God to lead people out of slavery. His followers called him a prophet.	Turner was captured after two months of evading the authorities. He was convicted and executed. This revolt resulted in widespread vigilante attacks by whites who killed an unknown number of enslaved and free African Americans. State governments also passed laws that further restricted enslaved peoples.
1839	A West African named **Cinque** led a mutiny of enslaved people against a Spanish slave ship, called the Amistad. They overpowered the crew and ordered them to sail them back to Africa. However, the captain sailed the ship to New York.	The Spanish demanded that the enslaved people be returned to them. The case was heard at the Supreme Court, where future president John Quincy Adams defended those enslaved. The enslaved people won their freedom.

1. Which revolt against slavery resulted in a positive outcome for the enslaved people?

    A. Nat Turner's revolt

    B. Denmark Vessey's plot

    C. the Amistad mutiny

    D. Charles Deslondes revolt

2. Who led a revolt that resulted in the government passing more strict laws regarding slavery?

    A. Charles Deslondes

    B. Gabriel Prosser

    C. Cinque

    D. Nat Turner

3. What do most of these revolts against slavery have in common?

_____

4. Why might the *Amistad* case be surprising?

_____

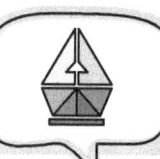
Directions: Read the text below. Then answer the questions that follow.

Enslaved people sought ways to escape oppression. Many escaped using the "**Underground Railroad**." This was not a real railroad but rather a secret network of people and routes that assisted enslaved people's escape. It operated from around the 1830s until the end of the Civil War. On the route, "conductors" guided enslaved people to "stations" or "safe houses" as they worked their way north. People who operated these stations were called "station masters." Most enslaved people fled to Canada since many northern states had laws that enforced the recapture of escaped enslaved people. It is thought that abround 100,000 enslaved people escaped using the Underground Railroad.

The most well-known conductor of the Underground Railroad was **Harriet Tubman** (1822-1913). She escaped slavery in Maryland in 1849 but returned to escort some 70 enslaved people to freedom on 13 trips back into Maryland. She said of her escape to freedom:

"I had crossed the line. I was free; but there was no one to welcome me to the land of freedom. I was a stranger in a strange land; and my home after all, was down in Maryland; because my father, my mother, my brothers, and sisters, and friends were there. But I was free, and they should be free."

1. What was the motivation for Harriet Tubman to return to Maryland?

....

....

2. What does the quote from Harriet Tubman indicate about what she gave up when she escaped slavery?

....

....

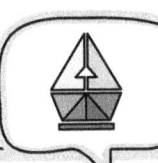
3. Based on your previous readings, what risks was Harriet Tubman making?

....

....

....

....

4. What does the Underground Railroad say about the experience of slavery?

....

....

....

....

....

....

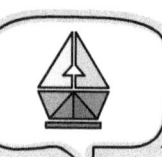
Directions: Read the text below. Then answer the questions that follow.

This week you learned about the growth of slavery in the United States before the Civil War. You also learned about how enslaved people resisted enslavement either through revolt or escape.

1. Describe the connection between the economy and slavery in the 19th century.

....

....

....

....

2. Elaborate on the common themes of uprisings against slavery in the 19th century.

....

....

....

....

3. How might the Underground Railroad, aside from being an escape route for enslaved people, also be a symbol for people who fought against slavery?

....

....

....

....

4. How was slavery hypocrital by the standard of American ideals?

....

....

....

....

Civics and Government

The Early Women's Rights Movement

This week, you will learn about the growth of reform movements in the early 19th century with a special emphasis on the development of the women's rights movement.

ARGOPREP

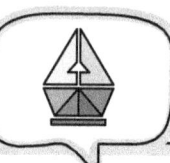
Directions: Read the text below. Then answer the questions that follow.

"

As slavery continued to grow in the South, many people began calling for reform and abolition. At the same time, an early women's rights movement was developing in the United States. The country had grown more democratic since the adoption of the Constitution. Initially, only white men with property could vote, but by the 1840s, most states had eliminated this requirement. At the same time, many states also instituted laws and restrictions that further limited the rights of free African Americans and women.

Calls for reform started from religious organizations that began to fight social problems, including reforming prisons, improving education, and calling for **temperance**, which was the banning of alcohol.

Prisons prior to this era were places of inhumane punishment. Reformers wanted to change prisons so that they reformed the convict rather than merely punishing them. By the 1860s, many states had changed prisons to penitentiaries. This turned the function of prisons from punishment to correction. Discipline, such as solitary confinement, was used in order to make convicts reflect on what they had done.

Education reform went hand in hand with the idea that a democratic republic needed public schools in order to have educated voters. Massachusetts politician **Horace Mann** led these efforts in his own state starting in the 1830s. The idea of tax-funded public schools became widely adopted in the northeast by the 1850s.

Temperance was another important social issue in the 19th century, as alcohol was widely used. Reformers believed that the misuse of alcohol led to poverty, abuse, crime, and other social evils.

The 19th century also marked the start of the rise of **abolitionists**, or those who sought to abolish slavery. Women at this time began taking active roles in the social reform movements of abolition and temperance. This eventually led to them fighting for their own rights as well.

"

1. Horace Mann is associated with what area of reform?

   A. prisons.

   B. temperance

   C. education

   D. abolitionism

2. How did democracy grow in the early 19th century?

    A. Property requirements were removed.

    B. Religious requirements were removed.

    C. Race requirements were removed.

    D. Sex requirements were removed.

3. What was the idea behind the introduction of penitentiaries?

    A. It was introduced to punish criminals rather than let them go free.

    B. It was introduced to reform criminals rather than punish them.

    C. It was introduced to educate people on the crimes caused by alcohol.

    D. It was introduced to inform people about the evils of slavery.

4. What was a justification for the establishment of public schools?

    A. They would improve the economy.

    B. They would promote a democratic republic.

    C. They would reform criminals.

    D. They would lower gender boundaries.

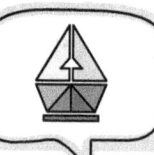
Directions: Read the text below. Then answer the questions that follow.

The movement for women's rights in many ways arose from the Industrial Revolution. Prior to industrialization, most families lived in rural, agricultural settings where everyone in a family lived and worked in the same place. When the place of work started to shift to factories or other places outside the home, the roles of men and women became different. Life became divided into two worlds - the realm of work and the realm of the home. It was thought that women were to remain at home to raise a moral family. Women were expected to be more pious and moral than men.

Because of these societal changes, white women became more and more involved in the moral reform movements of the 19th century. At the same time, white women began to call for their own equal treatment in society.

The first major call for equal rights for women occurred at the **Seneca Falls Convention** in New York in 1848. This Convention issued a "**Declaration of Rights and Sentiments**," which asserted that all men and women were equal. It called for women's **suffrage**, which is the right to vote. It also called for women to be allowed to hold and control property, serve on juries, sign legal documents, attend universities, and practice law and medicine.

Many **suffragists** supported the abolition of slavery, while others did not. Some supported abolition but believed that only white women should be able to vote. Sojourner Truth was a famous suffragist and abolitionist who was also formerly enslaved. She spread ideas about suffrage and equality for all women.

1. What did the *Declaration of Sentiments and Resolutions* call for?

   A. abolition of slavery

   B. job opportunities for women

   C. equal rights for women

   D. suffrage for African Americans

2. How was the early women's rights movement limited?

   A. It mainly centered around white women.

   B. It mainly was interested in temperance.

   C. It mainly was concerned with abolition.

   D. It mainly looked for property rights.

3. How did the Industrial Revolution influence the development of the women's rights movement?

....

....

....

....

....

4. Based on this passage, what rights were women fighting for?

....

....

....

....

....

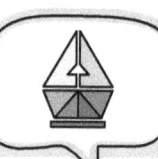
Directions: Read the text below. Then answer the questions that follow.

There were several prominent leaders of the early women's rights movement. These women served as role models for later generations in the struggle for women's equality. Here are some of the most prominent.

	Susan B. Anthony (1820-1906)	A major proponent of women's rights who worked in long partnership with Elizabeth Cady Stanton. She and Stanton would be the primary drivers for the women's suffrage movement in the later 19th century.
	Catharine Beecher (1800-1878)	An early education reformer from a prominent family, Beecher promoted the idea of women as a moral force.
	Elizabeth Blackwell (1821-1910)	Blackwell was the first woman to earn a medical degree in the United States. She founded a hospital in 1857 for women and children that was staffed just by women.

	Matilda Joslyn Gage (1826-1898)	Gage was a pioneer who argued that Christianity often worked to oppress women. She was an outspoken advocate for not just women's rights but the rights of Native Americans and African Americans.
	Lucretia Mott (1793-1880)	An early member of the abolitionist movement, Mott was influenced by her Quaker background which called for equality for all people. She collaborated with Elizabeth Cady Stanton for decades.
	Elizabeth Cady Stanton (1815-1902)	One of the primary leaders of the women's rights movement, she worked closely with Susan B. Anthony and Lucretia Mott in fighting for equal rights. She was the primary author of the *Declaration of Sentiments and Resolutions* from the Seneca Falls Convention.
	Sojourner Truth (1797-1883)	Born into slavery in New York but later freed, Sojourner Truth was an outspoken abolitionist who also pressed for women's rights.

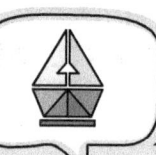
1. What is Elizabeth Blackwell known for?

   A. She helped to organize the Seneca Falls Convention.

   B. She was a strong proponent of the women's suffrage movement.

   C. She was formerly enslaved and was a strong abolitionist.

   D. She was the first woman to receive a medical degree in the United States.

2. Which reformer was an early promoter of the idea of women as a moral force?

   A. Catharine Beecher

   B. Sojourner Truth

   C. Matilda Joslyn Gage

   D. Susan B. Anthony

3. Which reformer argued that Christianity often led to further oppression of women?

   A. Matilda Joslyn Gage

   B. Elizabeth Cady Stanton

   C. Lucretia Mott

   D. Elizabeth Blackwell

4. What is unique about Sojourner Truth when compared to other reformers?

   A. She was from the South.

   B. She was formerly enslaved.

   C. She argued for women's suffrage.

   D. She had a Quaker background.

Directions: Read the text below. Then answer the questions that follow.

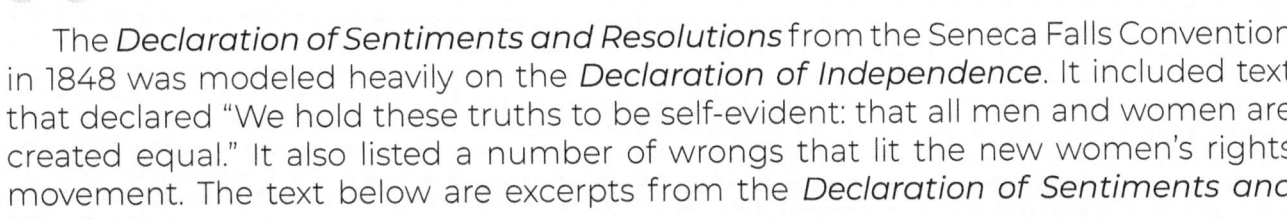

The *Declaration of Sentiments and Resolutions* from the Seneca Falls Convention in 1848 was modeled heavily on the *Declaration of Independence*. It included text that declared "We hold these truths to be self-evident: that all men and women are created equal." It also listed a number of wrongs that lit the new women's rights movement. The text below are excerpts from the *Declaration of Sentiments and Resolutions*:

The history of mankind is a history of repeated injuries and usurpations on the part of man toward woman, having in direct object the establishment of an absolute tyranny over her. To prove this, let facts be submitted to a candid world.

* *He has never permitted her to exercise her inalienable right to the elective franchise.*

* *He has compelled her to submit to laws, in the formation of which she had no voice.*

* *He has withheld from her rights which are given to the most ignorant and degraded men—both natives and foreigners.*

* *He has made her, if married, in the eye of the law, civilly dead.*

* *He has taken from her all right in property, even to the wages she earns.*

* *He has monopolized nearly all the profitable employments, and from those she is permitted to follow, she receives but a scanty remuneration.*

* *He closes against her all the avenues to wealth and distinction, which he considers most honorable to himself. As a teacher of theology, medicine, or law, she is not known.*

* *He has denied her the facilities for obtaining a thorough education—all colleges being closed against her.*

1. According to the text, what rights did the *Declaration of Sentiments and Resolutions* state were being denied to women?

....

....

....

....

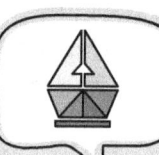
2. In your view, which of the rights listed in the text is most important? Explain why.

....

....

....

....

3. Which of the complaints in the *Declaration of Sentiments and Resolutions* have been resolved?

....

....

....

....

4. Which of the complaints in the *Declaration of Sentiments and Resolutions* are still issues today?

....

....

....

....

....

....

Directions: Read the text below. Then answer the questions that follow.

This week you learned about the growth of reform movements in the early 19th century with a special focus on the beginnings of the women's rights movement.

1. How did education reform promote a democratic society?

2. Describe how religion played a factor in the development of the women's rights movement.

3. How was the women's rights movement linked to the abolitionist movement?

4. How was the early women's rights movement limited?

Geography

America Divides and Compromises

FREE STATE

SLAVE STATE

This week, you will learn about the growth of abolitionism and the political compromises which were made to hold the United States together over the issue of slavery.

ARGOPREP

Directions: Read the text below. Then answer the questions that follow.

Slavery was the most debated and controversial issue in the United States during the first half of the 19th century. As you learned about in previous weeks, slavery was at odds with the concepts of liberty and equality at the heart of founding of the United States. Those who opposed slavery saw it as a moral evil. As a result, there were movements early on to ban it. Shortly after independence, most states in the North began to gradually emancipate, or free, enslaved people. Pennsylvania began this process in 1780. In New York, enslaved people were gradually **emancipated** between 1799 and 1827. In 1781 a Massachusetts judge ruled that slavery went against the principles of the state's constitution. In 1808, Congress banned the importation of enslaved people from overseas into any state. However, states in the South maintained their slave populations through laws that said anyone born into slavery was enslaved themselves.

Gradual, state-by-state emancipation stood in contrast to the desires of **abolitionsists** who wanted an immediate end to slavery. One of the first prominent abolitionists was **William Lloyd Garrison** who established the anti-slavery newspaper, the Liberator, in 1831. Another was **Frederick Douglass** who was born into slavery in Maryland but escaped. Another well-known abolitionist was **Harriett Beecher Stowe** who wrote *Uncle Tom's Cabin*. Published in 1852, this popular book was at the center of controversy for its negative portrayals of life in slavery. Harriet Tubman, who you have learned was a conductor for the Underground Railroad, was also an outspoken abolitionist.

Abolitionists were often seen as radicals, especially in the pro-slavery states. Others argued that slavery should end, but that freed African Americans should return to Africa. These sentiments were seen in the creation of the **American Colonization Society** in 1817, which established Liberia on the west coast of Africa as a haven for formerly enslaved people. However, most free African Americans viewed the United States as their home and did not wish to leave.

1. Which abolitionist founded the *Liberator*?

   A. Harriett Tubman

   B. Harriet Beecher Stowe

   C. William Lloyd Garrison

   D. Frederick Douglass

THE LIBERATOR

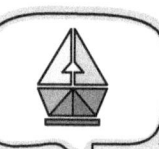
2. The American Colonization Society sought to

A. gradually emancipate enslaved people.

B. take control of the international slave trade.

C. expand slavery by establishing new colonies.

D. resettle formerly enslaved people out of the country.

3. How did Massachusetts effectively end slavery?

A. by court order

B. by constitutional amendment

C. by passage of laws

D. by economic forces

4. How did most states in the North deal with slavery after the American Revolution?

A. They banned it outright.

B. They got rid of it slowly.

C. They expanded it.

D. They limited it the slave trade.

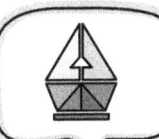
Directions: Read the text below. Then answer the questions that follow.

As the United States expanded, the issue of slavery grew to become one that threatened to destroy the country as a whole. The country started growing apart economically and socially. Industrialization and reform flourished in the North, while an economy dependent on agriculture and enslaved labor grew in the South. In the North, the abolition movement had taken root and was demanding an end to slavery, while in the South the economy depended on it. Southerners believed that any assault on slavery was an assault on private property. The country became divided into Southern slave states and northern free states. People began to feel more loyalty to their section of the country rather than the country as a whole. This was called **sectionalism**.

Meanwhile, in Congress, due to a growing population, representatives from northern states gained control of the majority of the House of Representatives. But because each state was given two senators, there was a delicate balance of power in the Senate. Politicians tried to maintain this balance. However, as calls for the end of slavery continued, there was the question of what would happen to territories in the West as they became states.

The first crisis appeared in 1820 when Missouri applied for admission into the Union as a slave state. In order to maintain a balance of power, Senator Henry Clay of Kentucky brokered the **Missouri Compromise** to keep both free and slave states satisfied. It allowed Missouri to enter the Union as a slave state and Maine to break off from Massachusetts and enter as a free state. Any new states that were admitted later that were south of a certain line of latitude would allow slavery. Those to the north of the line would be free states.

However, this was only a temporary solution. After the annexation of Texas and the territory from Mexico, the issue of slavery arose again. In 1850, Henry Clay brokered the **Compromise of 1850**. This compromise admitted California as a free state and allowed New Mexico and Utah to decide for themselves on the issue of slavery through a concept called **popular sovereignty**. The Compromise also banned the slave trade in Washington, D.C. To appease southern states, a new **Fugitive Slave Act** was passed that provided greater enforcement for the capture of escaped enslaved people. This was because the South had trouble recovering escaped enslaved people from northern states. These compromises were meant to keep a balance of power so the country could stay united. However, these compromises only delayed the conflict.

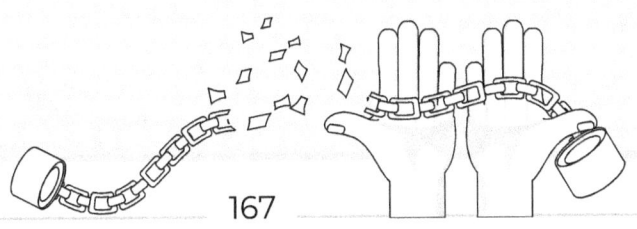

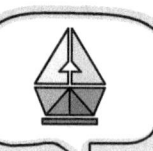
1. The Missouri Compromise included which of the following elements?
   A. the admission of California as a slave state
   B. a ban on the slave trade in the capital
   C. a new law to capture escaped enslaved people
   D. the creation of the state of Maine

2. The purpose of the compromises over slavery was to
   A. protect private property.
   B. control the institution of slavery.
   C. maintain a balance of power in the Senate.
   D. admit new states to the Union.

3. The driving force that resulted in the Missouri Compromise and Compromise of 1850 was
   A. the acquisition of new lands in the West.
   B. the industrialization of the North.
   C. the growth of slavery in the South.
   D. the rise of the abolition movement.

4. What demographic change weakened the South's political power?
   A. increasing industrial growth in the North.
   B. settlement of lands in the West
   C. rising enslaved people population in the South
   D. growing population in the North.

FREE STATE   SLAVE STATE

Directions: Study the maps below. Then answer the questions that follow.

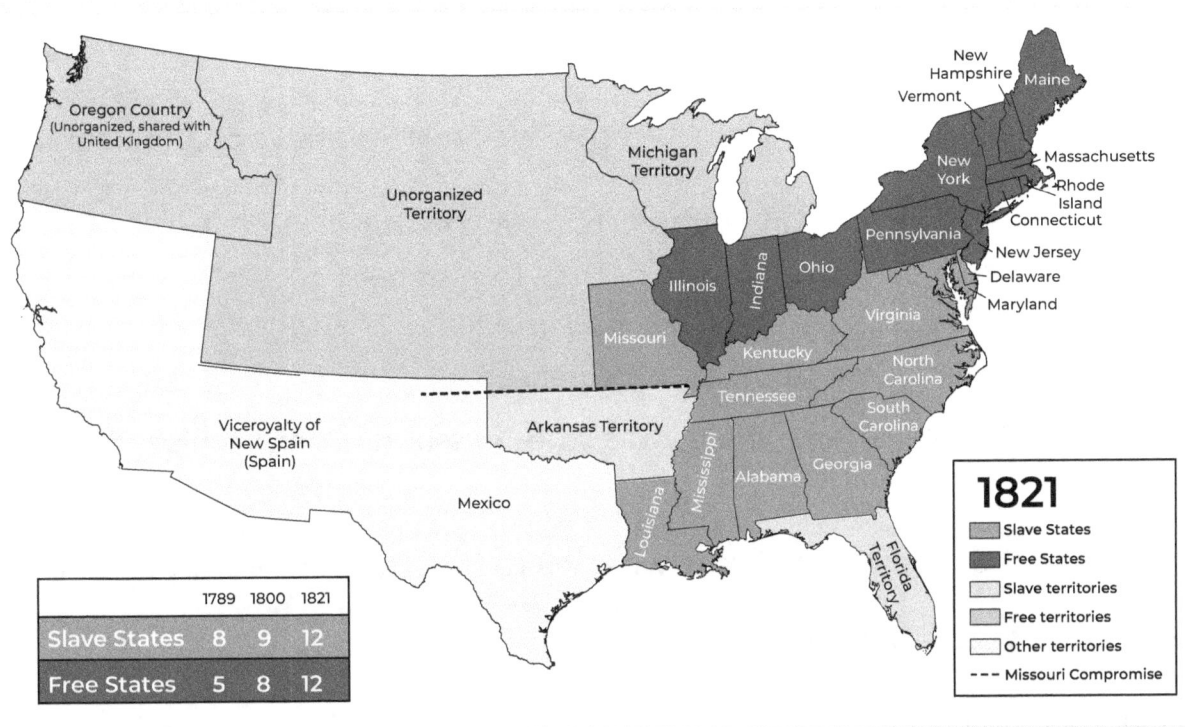

1821

- Slave States
- Free States
- Slave territories
- Free territories
- Other territories
- --- Missouri Compromise

	1789	1800	1821
Slave States	8	9	12
Free States	5	8	12

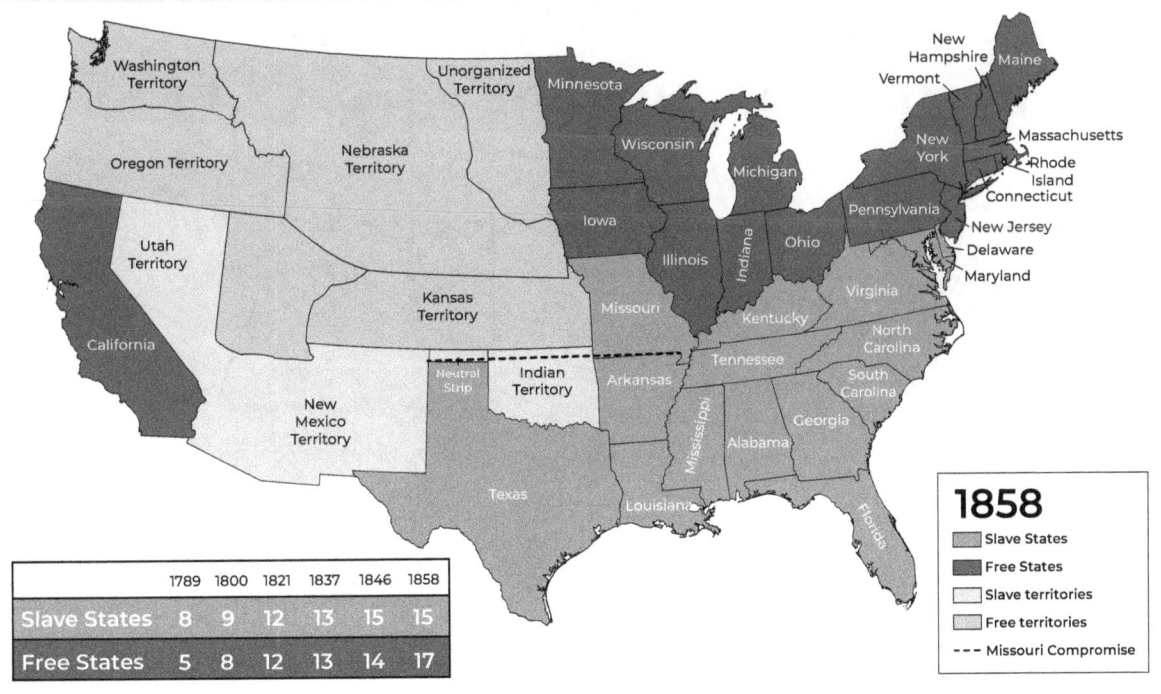

1858

- Slave States
- Free States
- Slave territories
- Free territories
- --- Missouri Compromise

	1789	1800	1821	1837	1846	1858
Slave States	8	9	12	13	15	15
Free States	5	8	12	13	14	17

1. What territory did the United States control in 1858 that it did not in 1821?
   A. Nebraska territory
   B. Missouri
   C. California
   D. Kansas territory

2. How did the balance of power between slave and free states change between 1821 and 1858?
   A. Free states grew more in number than slave states.
   B. Slave states grew more in number than free states.
   C. Free states and slave states remained equal.
   D. Slave states and free states both decreased.

3. According to the map where was the Missouri Compromise line located?

   ....

4. According the map, do you live in what was a free state or territory in 1821?

   What state or territory was it? ....

   What about in 1858? ....

Directions: Read the text below. Then answer the questions that follow.

The following passage is an excerpt of a speech delivered by Senator John C. Calhoun of South Carolina in 1837:

We of the South will not, cannot surrender our institutions. To maintain the existing relations between the two races, inhabiting [the South], is indispensable to the peace and happiness of both. It cannot be [undermined] without drenching the county in blood, and [eliminating] one or the other of the races. Be it good or bad, it has grown up with our society and institutions, and is so interwoven with them, that to destroy it would be to destroy us as a people.

But let me not be understood as admitting, even by implication, that the existing relations between the two races in the slaveholding States is an evil: - far otherwise; I hold it to be a good, as it has thus far proved itself to be to both, and will continue to be so if not disturbed by the fell spirit of abolition.

I appeal to facts. Never before has the black race of Central Africa, from the dawn of history to the present day, attained a condition so civilized and so improved, not only physically, but morally and intellectually. It came among us in a low, degraded, and savage condition, and in the course of a few generations it has grown up under the fostering care of our institutions, reviled as they have been, to its present comparatively civilized condition. This, with the rapid increase of numbers, is conclusive proof of the general happiness of the race, in spite of all the exaggerated tales to the contrary.

1. Summarize Calhoun's argument.

_____

_____

2. What assumptions is Calhoun making in this speech?

_____

_____

3. How is Calhoun measuring enslaved people's happiness in this passage?

_____

_____

4. What does Calhoun warn of if slavery is interefered with?

_____

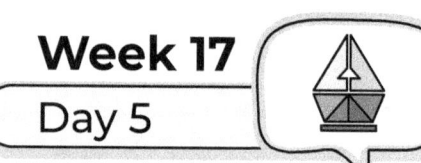
Directions: Read the text below. Then answer the questions that follow.

This week you learned about the rising abolitionist movement and the political compromises made between slave and free states in order to maintain the Union.

1. How did the expansion of the country make the fight over slavery worse?

....

....

....

....

2. What assumptions were movements such as the American Colonization Society making about free African Americans?

....

....

....

....

3. How did sectionalism demonstrate the growing divisions in the United States?

....

....

....

....

....

WEEK 18

History
The Crisis Deepens

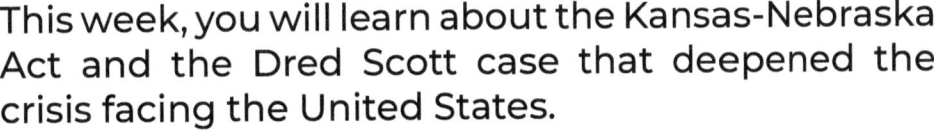

This week, you will learn about the Kansas-Nebraska Act and the Dred Scott case that deepened the crisis facing the United States.

ARGOPREP

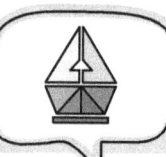
Directions: Read the text below. Then answer the questions that follow.

As you learned last week, Congress compromised to keep a balance of power between slave and free states. In the meantime, the controversy over slavery continued to grow. As part of Henry Clay's Compromise of 1850, Congress enacted a stronger **Fugitive Slave Act**. Under this act, any African American, free or enslaved, could be accused of being a runaway, captured, and ruled on by a commissioner who received a $10 fee if they favored the slaveholder as opposed to only $5 if they favored the accused. It also required that regular citizens were required to help capture runaways. Many Northerners worked against the act, continuing to run and expand the Underground Railroad.

The act, which Clay had thought would help the South actually had the effect of deepening divisions. It was in this context that the issue of the organization of western lands came up again. Unorganized territory needed to be organized in order to accommodate plans for a transcontinental railroad that could connect the eastern states to California and other Pacific coast territories. Senator Stephen A. Douglas of Illinois proposed a plan to organize these territories as Nebraska. Since the territory was north of the Missouri Compromise line it would be free territory. Southern senators refused to agree to it unless the Missouri Compromise was repealed. Douglas, therefore, proposed the **Kansas-Nebraska Act** which repealed the Missouri Compromise and divided the territory into Nebraska in the north and Kansas in the south. In both territories, citizens would vote on whether to allow or ban slavery. This is an example of **popular sovereignty**, which was used in the Compromise of 1850. Despite much opposition by anti-slavery forces, the bill passed in 1854, setting the stage for the first act of violence before the Civil War.

1. What was the impact of the Fugitive Slave Act on Northern opinion?

   A. It created an atmosphere of compliance.

   B. It helped strengthen popular sovereignty.

   C. It strengthened anti-slavery opinon.

   D. It helped support for western territory reorganization.

2. What is popular sovereignty?

    A. It required the population of free states to assist in the recapture of enslaved people.

    B. It revoked prior compromises over slavery by allowing it to apply to the entire population.

    C. It is a means by which the people of a state would decide for themselves on the issue of slavery.

    D. It was the plan to connect the United States from coast to coast with a new railroad.

3. To organize western territories, what did Stephen A. Douglas propose?

    A. that the Missouri Compromise line be extended

    B. that the voters decide on the issue of slavery

    C. that slavery be allowed throughout the territories

    D. that slavery be banned throughout the territories

4. For free African Americans, why was the Fugitive Slave Act unfair?

    A. because the act subjected them to capture

    B. because the act denied them the right to vote

    C. because the act levied heavy fines on them

    D. because the act declared they were not citizens

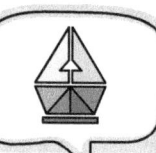
Directions: Read the text below. Then answer the questions that follow.

"

The Kansas-Nebraska Act of 1854 declared that voters would decide on the issue of slavery in the territories of Kansas and Nebraska. This issue became of national importance, since the balance of power in the Senate depended on whether the state was slave or free. As a result, Northern abolitionists hurried into Kansas in order to make it a free territory. In response, thousands of pro-slavery Missourians, called "**border ruffians**," headed into the territory. These Missourians voted illegally to create a pro-slavery legislature. The anti-slavery forces then held their own convention and established a second government that banned slavery.

Violence broke out in May 1856 with border ruffians attacking the town of Lawrence, which was a stronghold for anti-slavery forces. Fighting continued so that by the end of the year about 200 were dead. Most notable in these fights was the fervent abolitionist **John Brown** who, with his sons, killed five pro-slavery partisans. Kansas came to be known as "**Bleeding Kansas**."

Brown's attack was in part set off because of a violent incident in the Senate. On May 19, 1856, the abolitionist Senator **Charles Sumner** made a speech about the conflict in Kansas that targeted Senator **Andrew Butler** of South Carolina. The speech was inflammatory, and Butler's nephew, Representative **Preston Brooks** took revenge on Sumner two days later by beating him in the Senate chambers with his cane. Sumner was badly injured and the attack strengthened Northern sentiment against the South while Brooks was hailed as a Southern hero.

Anger over the Kansas-Nebraska Act caused the **Whig** Party, one of the two major political parties, to disintegrate. This resulted in the formation of a new party, the **Republican Party**, in 1854. Republicans did not all agree that slavery should be abolished, but they did agree that slavery should be kept out of the territories.

John Brown

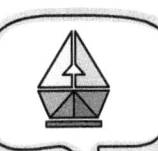

1. Who were the border ruffians?

   A. armed troops sent to stop violence in Kansas

   B. citizens of Kansas who had settled in the territory

   C. anti-slavery partisans who used violence in Kansas

   D. pro-slavery people from Missouri who entered Kansas

2. Which abolitionist attacked and killed pro-slavery forces in Lawrence, Kansas?

   A. John Brown

   B. Charles Sumner

   C. Andrew Butler

   D. Preston Brooks

3. Which senator was beaten on the Senate floor due to an abolitionist speech he made?

   A. Preston Brooks

   B. John Brown

   C. Charles Sumner

   D. Andrew Butler

4. What political party disappeared as a result of the Kansas-Nebraska Act?

   A. Republicans

   B. Whigs

   C. Federalists

   D. Democrats

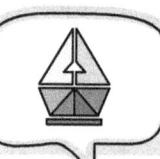
Directions: Study the text below. Then answer the questions that follow.

"

Tensions between the North and South had grown intense since the Kansas-Nebraska Act. The Dred Scott v. Sandford case of 1857 was another conflict that propelled America toward war.

President **James Buchanan** came into office in 1857 and wanted to settle the question of slavery. He encouraged the Supreme Court to take up a case on the issue. That case came when Dred Scott filed suit. Dred Scott was an enslaved man who lived in Missouri under his slaveowner. The slaveowner had relocated temporarily to free territory, took Scott and then returned to Missouri. Abolitionists helped Dred Scott file a lawsuit which claimed that since he had spent time in free territory, he was free.

The Supreme Court Chief Justice **Roger B. Taney** issued the majority opinion in a 7-2 ruling. He dismissed the case, stating that African Americans, free or enslaved, were not citizens, and therefore Dred Scott could not sue. Taney also stated that the ban on slavery north of the Missouri Compromise line was unconstitutional since Congress did not have the power to ban slavery in the territories.

The decision was hailed by slave states while Republicans roundly denounced it. Taney had probably, like President Buchanan, wanted to settle the issue. However, it inflamed tensions as never before. One of the leading denouncers of the *Dred Scott* decision was **Abraham Lincoln**, a rising figure in the Republican Party. Lincoln saw the decision as a plot to expand slavery throughout the country.

"

1. Which of the following was part of Roger B. Taney's opinion in the Dred Scott decision?

   A. that enslaved people had the right to sue

   B. That enslaved people could not move to free territory

   C. the Missouri Compromise was constitutional

   D. that African Americans were not citizens

2. How did Abraham Lincoln view the *Dred Scott* decision?

   A. that it was a plot to expand slavery

   B. that it was reasonably argued

   C. that free states should support the decision

   D. that it would start war

3. What did Roger B. Taney declare as unconstitutional in the *Dred Scott* decision?

....

....

....

4. What was President Buchanan's intent with encouraging a Supreme Court ruling?

....

....

....

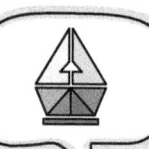
Directions: Read the text below. Then answer the questions that follow.

"

The caning of Senator Charles Sumner on the Senate floor by Representative Preston Brooks showed just how divided the country had become. Northerners spoke out against the attack, while some Southerners sent Preston Brooks more canes to show solidarity. Below is a political cartoon of the attack which circulated widely.

SOUTHERN CHIVALRY — ARGUMENT versus CLUB'S.

"

1. Who is the cartoon supporting, Brooks or Sumner? Why?

....

....

....

....

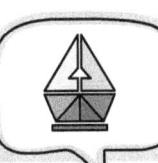
2. What do you think the caption on the cartoon signifies?

....

....

....

....

3. How might this cartoon have changed public opinion in the North?

....

....

....

....

....

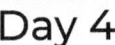

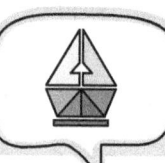
Directions: Read the text below. Then answer the questions that follow.

This week you learned about the crises that led the country down the road to civil war.

1. Elaborate on how the Fugitive Slave Act created resentment toward the South by the North.

....

....

....

....

2. "Bleeding Kansas" is sometimes called a prelude to the Civil War. Why is this?

....

....

....

....

3. In a speech in 1858 Abraham Lincoln stated:

A house divided against itself cannot stand. I believe this government cannot endure, permanently half slave and half free. I do not expect the Union to be dissolved - I do not expect the house to fall - but I do expect it will cease to be divided. It will become all one thing, or all the other.

Elaborate on what Lincoln means.

....

....

....

....

....

History

The Civil War Begins

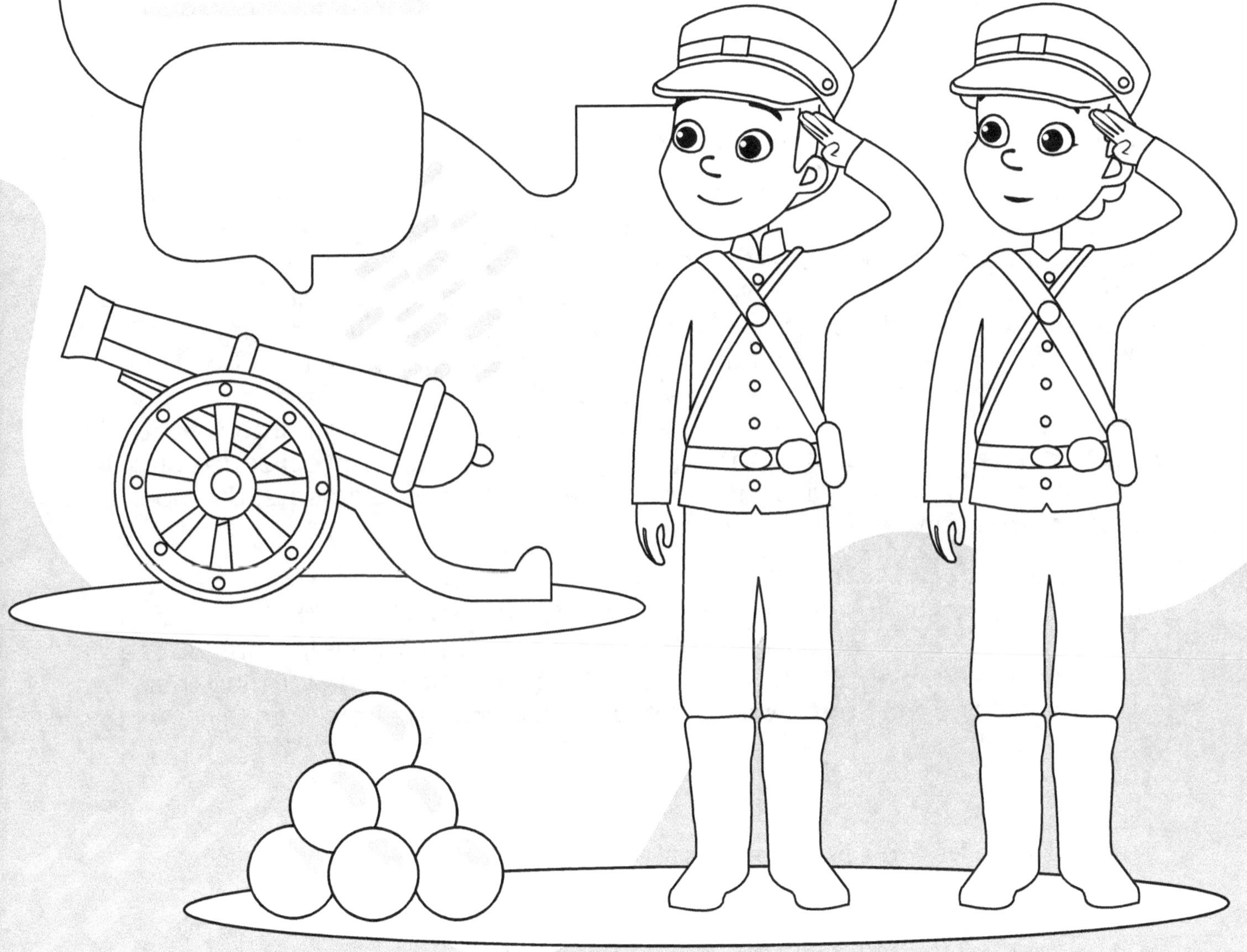

This week, you will learn about the causes of the Civil War and the relative strengths and weaknesses of the North and South. You will also learn about Abraham Lincoln and the Emancipation Proclamation.

ARGOPREP

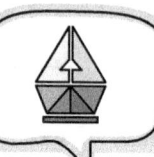
Directions: Read the text below. Then answer the questions that follow.

By the late 1850s, the United States was on the brink of civil war. The growing anti-slavery movement and the South's determination to defend the institution led to such deep differences that it was beyond the point of compromise.

In October 1859, the abolitionist John Brown, who had taken a prominent role in the violence of "Bleeding Kansas," attempted to seize the federal arsenal at **Harpers Ferry**, Virginia. He planned to arm enslaved people with weapons from the arsenal in order to bring about a massive rebellion. He was captured within 36 hours and put on trial. At the trial, Brown said, "The crimes of this guilty land will never be purged away but with blood." Brown was executed. He became a martyr in the North and was vilified in the South. The country was ready to go to war over slavery.

The tipping point that led to the start of the Civil War was the **presidential election of 1860**. In this election, the Democratic party was torn apart over the slavery debate. Southern Democrats who wanted a full endorsement of slavery split off from Northern Democrats who supported popular sovereignty. In the end, the Northern Democrats nominated Stephen A. Douglas, while the Southern Democrats ran John C. Breckinridge. A new political party made up of former Whigs, the Constitutional Union Party, nominated John Bell; they feared the country was going to fall apart. These party divisions benefitted the Republican candidate, Abraham Lincoln, who won a plurality of the popular vote and a majority of the electoral college. A **plurality** occurs when a candidate wins more votes than any other candidate, but does not constitute a majority vote.

With Lincoln elected, the South viewed their entire way of life as threatened. Lincoln tried to assure the South, but it was too late. Starting with South Carolina, the states in the South voted to **secede**, or leave, the Union. By February 1861, seven states had left the Union. By May 1861, 11 states had left the Union, forming their own government called the **Confederate States of America**. The American Civil War had begun.

1. Why did John Brown seize the federal arsenal at Harpers Ferry, Virginia?

   A. He was trying to prevent a civil war.

   B. He objected to the results of the election of 1860.

   C. He was following orders from Confederate leaders.

   D. He wanted to start a revolt of enslaved people.

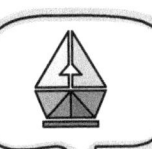
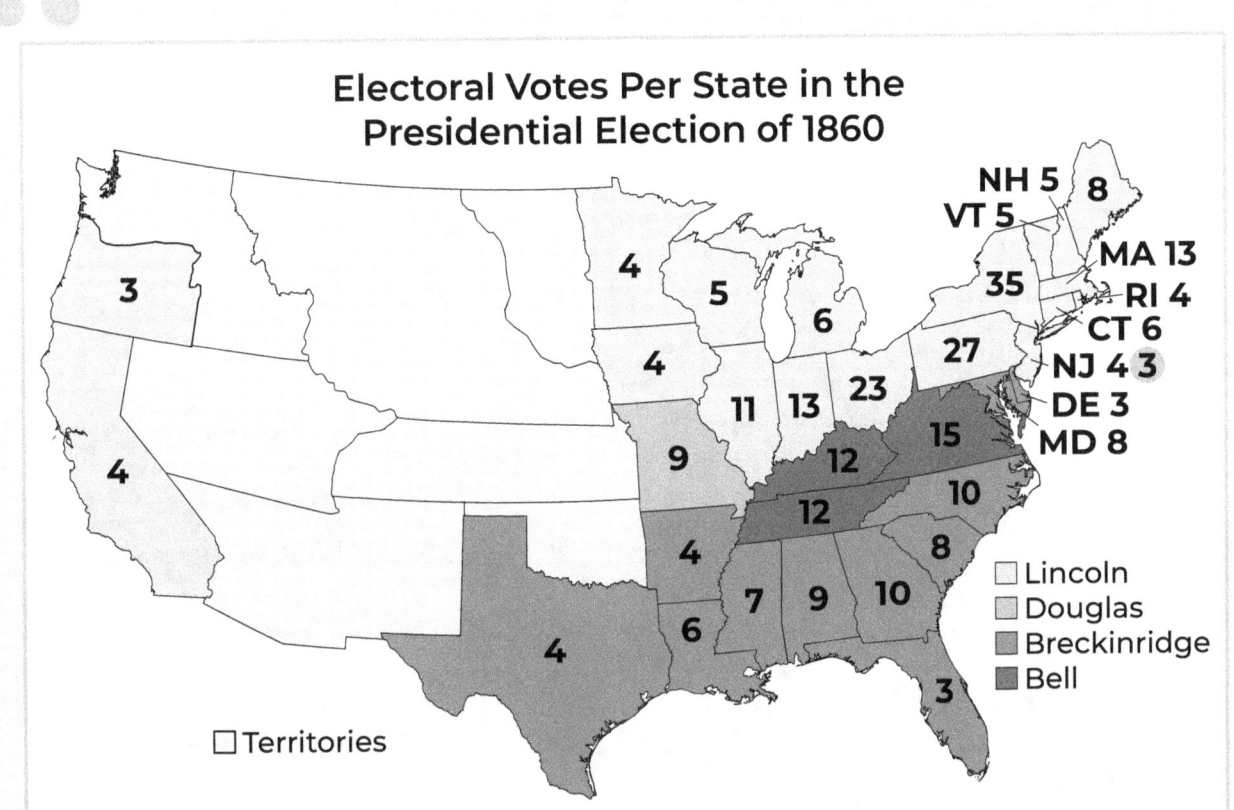

Electoral Votes Per State in the Presidential Election of 1860

Lincoln
Douglas
Breckinridge
Bell

Territories

2. What was the immediate event that resulted in the secession of Southern states from the Union?

   A. the attack of a federal fort

   B. the results of a presidential election

   C. the seizure of a federal arsenal

   D. the violence over slavery in western territories

3. How did a split in the Democratic party impact Abraham Lincoln?

   A. It allowed him to win more votes than other candidates.

   B. It took away important votes in the South from him.

   C. It led to a violent election that led directly to war.

   D. It made him unite with other democrats.

4. According to the map in this section, where were most of the states that voted for Abraham Lincoln?

   A. East   **B.** West   **C.** South   **D.** North

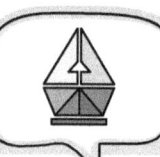
Directions: Read the text below. Then answer the questions that follow.

The American Civil War pitted the North against the South. The first fighting occurred from April 12 to 13, 1861 when South Carolina attacked **Fort Sumter** in Charleston Harbor. Abraham Lincoln called for 75,000 volunteers to serve in the military. This call resulted in states in the Upper South, including Virginia, seceding from the Union. In terms of resources, the North was substantially stronger, as the table below shows.

	North	South
Population	21 million	9 million (3.5 of which were enslaved)
Railroad mileage	22,000	9,000
Value of manufactured goods	$1.7 billion	$156 million
Corn and wheat production (bushels)	698 million	314 million
Bank deposits	$207 million	$47 million

The Confederacy could not hope to win a long war against the Union because of the North's superior resources. However, this did not mean that the South's rebellion was doomed to fail. The Confederacy hoped that either the North would accept the South's secession or that the South would receive support from foreign governments. Therefore, the Confederate president, **Jefferson Davis**, wanted to wage a **defensive war** in order to make the North tired of war and come to terms with the status quo. This gave the South the advantage of not having to outright defeat Union troops but simply to continue to harass them. The South also had the advantage of having very able generals, such as **Robert E. Lee** and **Thomas "Stonewall" Jackson**, who left their positions in the federal army to join the Confederate cause.

1. What advantage did the Confederacy have in the Civil War?

    A. more financial strength

    B. home advantage

    C. more railroads

    D. higher population

2. What was the general strategy of the Confederacy?

    A. to take over the North militarily

    B. to have the North accept their secession

    C. to blockade Northern ports

    D. to use their economic strength to defeat the North

3. Fort Sumter, South Carolina is notable because

    A. it was a central military facility of the Union.

    B. it was commanded by General Robert E. Lee.

    C. it was where the first fighting of the Civil War took place.

    D. it was where foreign governments first intervened in the war.

4. Who was the president of the Confederacy?

    A. Jefferson Davis

    B. Robert E. Lee

    C. Thomas Jackson

    D. Abraham Lincoln

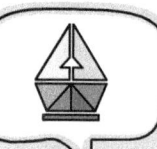
Directions: Read the text below. Then answer the questions that follow.

Both sides of the Civil War expected a quick fight and resolution. In July 1861, in the first major battle of the war at Bull Run, also called the **Battle of Manassas**, Confederate troops defeated Union troops. It became clear that this was going to be a long war. This led to Lincoln calling for the enlistment of 500,000 troops to help defeat the Confederacy. These men were volunteers, but as the war dragged on, fewer men were willing to volunteer to fight. Both sides, therefore, began drafting men to serve in their armies. Drafting people into the army is also called **conscription**. Early in the war, the Union suffered losses putting the Union on the defensive in the East. The Confederate General Robert E. Lee, then took up a strategy of trying to invade the North. The idea was that a successful invasion would help bring about foreign support. The British government was considering it, but in September 1862, the Union forced Lee to retreat at the **Battle of Antietam**. Antietam was the bloodiest one-day battle in American history, with some 6,000 soldiers killed and 17,000 wounded. Lee began to prepare to campaign deep into Union territory.

At this point, the Union wasn't doing so well in the East. In the West, the Union was seeing victories under General Ulysses S. Grant. The North's objective was to get control of the Mississippi River, which was a vital supply route to the South. In addition, the Union Navy began a blockade of all southern ports. Even though the South was able to get blockade runners through, the blockade had the effect of ruining the Confederate economy.

Meanwhile, on September 22, 1862, Abraham Lincoln issued the Emancipation Proclamation. He declared that as of January 1, 1863, all enslaved people in states that were in rebellion would be free. Unfortunately, Lincoln didn't have the power to liberate enslaved people in the Confederacy, since he was no longer in power there. However, he did free a significant number of enslaved people in states that remained in the Union. Regardless, the **Emancipation Proclamation** was important because it turned the objective of the war from preserving the union to liberating enslaved people. It also allowed newly freed African Americans to enlist in the Union army.

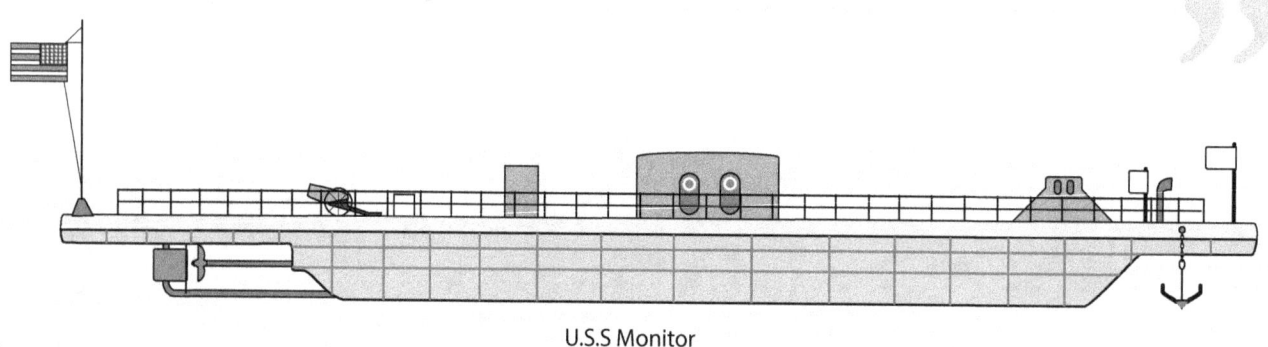

U.S.S Monitor

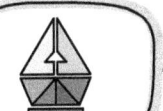
1. Which battle was the bloodiest one-day fight in American history?

   A. Antietam

   B. Sumter

   C. Bull Run

   D. Manassas

2. What is conscription?

   A. volunteering to serve in the military

   B. requiring people to serve in the military

   C. freeing people who are in occupied areas

   D. declaring martial law in a region

3. What did the Emancipation Proclamation do?

....

....

....

....

4. How did the Union use its Navy?

....

....

....

....

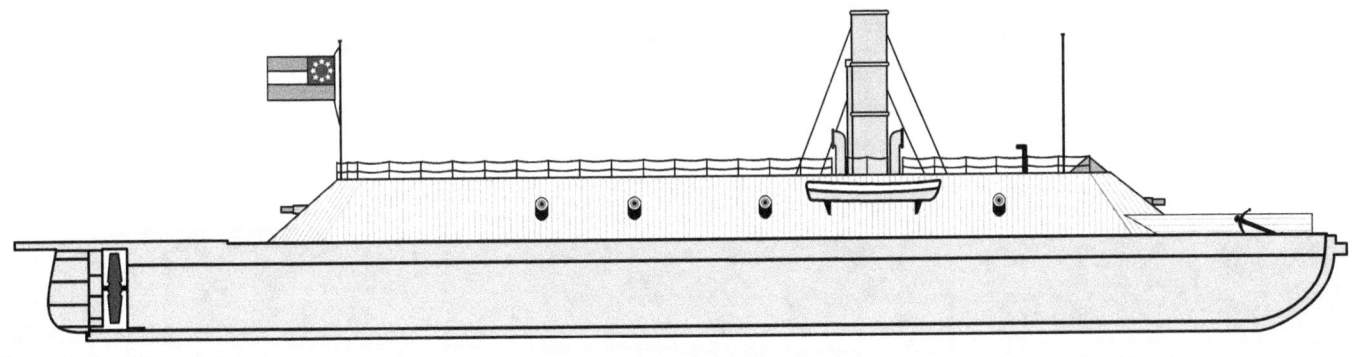

CSS Virginia

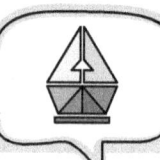
Directions: Read the text below. Then answer the questions that follow.

The following passage is an excerpt from a letter from Abraham Lincoln dated August 22, 1862, just before he issued the Emancipation Proclamation:

"If there be those who would not save the Union unless they could at the same time save slavery, I do not agree with them. If there be those who would not save the Union unless they could at the same time destroy slavery, I do not agree with them. My paramount object in this struggle is to save the Union, and is not either to save or to destroy slavery. If I could save the Union without freeing any slave I would do it, and if I could save it by freeing all the slaves I would do it; and if I could save it by freeing some and leaving others alone, I would also do that. What I do about slavery and the colored race, I do because I believe it helps to save the Union; and what I forbear [choose not to do], I forbear because I do not believe it would help to save the Union. "

1. What position is Abraham Lincoln taking in this letter toward abolition?

....

....

....

....

....

2. What could be a reason why Lincoln chooses to take this position?

....

....

....

....

....

Directions: Read the text below. Then answer the questions that follow.

This week you learned about the beginning of the Civil War, the strengths and weaknesses of the North and the South, as well as the Emancipation Proclamation.

1. What were the relative strengths and weaknesses of the North and the South?

2. How did Robert E. Lee's strategy conflict with the South's overall strategy of a defensive war?

3. Why do you think Abraham Lincoln limited the Emancipation Proclamation to only states that were in rebellion?

WEEK 20

History

The War Between the States

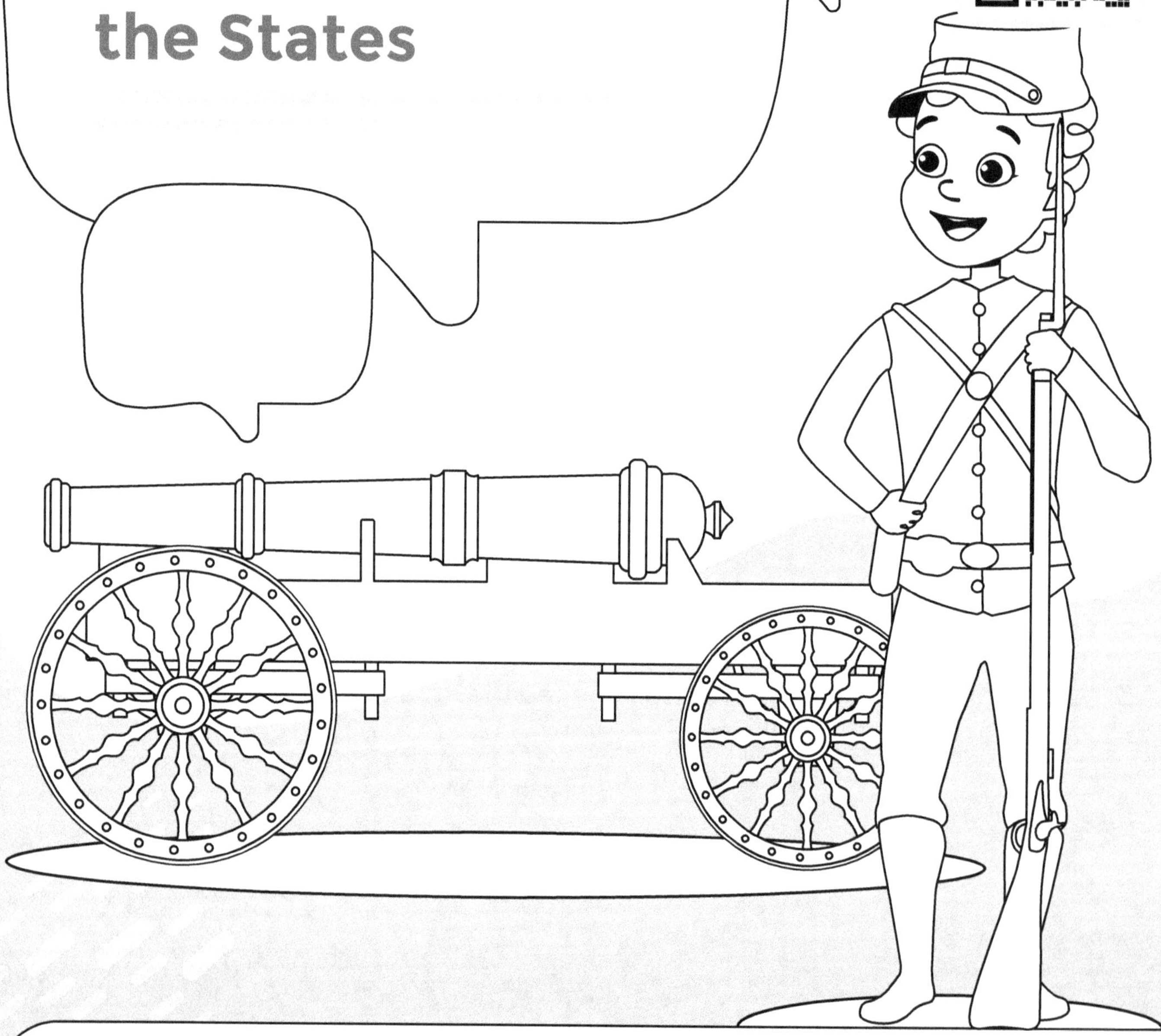

This week, you will learn about the fighting of the Civil War and how it permanently changed the country.

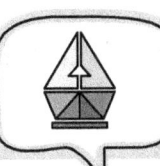
Directions: Read the text below. Then answer the questions that follow.

The American Civil War was the bloodiest conflict in American history. Approximately 620,000 men died either fighting for the Union or the Confederacy. The next bloodiest conflict was World War II, which saw about 405,000 deaths.

As you learned last week, the early days of the war were inconclusive. The Confederates had won some major battles under the leadership of Robert E. Lee, who took on a strategy to invade northern territories. Lee hoped to force the Union to the bargaining table and help promote foreign recognition of the Confederacy. Meanwhile, the Union was trying to weaken the Confederacy through a naval blockade as well as by gaining control of the Mississippi River.

The turning point in the conflict came in July 1863. First, Union troops under the command of **Ulysses S. Grant** laid siege to the strategically important city of Vicksburg, Mississippi. Grant took the city on July 4, 1863, a move that greatly prevented the flow of supplies and troops throughout the Confederacy. The second turning point was the **Battle of Gettysburg**. General Lee led his troops into Pennsylvania to seize supplies. At Gettysburg, Lee met the Union army under the command of General **George Meade**. Between July 1 and July 5, the two forces battled. The Union emerged victorious. Over 7,000 had been killed and another 33,000 wounded.

After Gettysburg, there was no chance that the Confederacy could gain foreign recognition or seriously vie with the Union on the battlefield. For the rest of the war, the Confederacy was on the defensive. General Grant was appointed by Lincoln as the chief general of the Union forces, and he returned east where he faced off against Lee. It took another two years of heavy fighting for Lee to finally surrender to Grant at **Appomattox Courthouse**, Virginia on April 9, 1865.

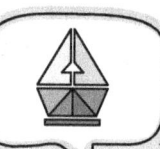
1. Why did the Confederate army enter Gettysburg?
   - **A.** They were attempting to gain control of a water route.
   - **B.** They were trying to outflank the Union army.
   - **C.** They were hoping to seize supplies.
   - **D.** They were seeking a safe refuge.

2. Which general was in charge of the Union's forces at Gettysburg?
   - **A.** George Meade
   - **B.** Ulysses S. Grant
   - **C.** William Tecumseh Sheridan
   - **D.** Robert E. Lee

3. Why was the siege of Vicksburg, Mississippi a turning point in the war?
   - **A.** It stopped advances of Confederate troops into Union territory.
   - **B.** It blocked the flow of troops and supplies in the Confederacy.
   - **C.** It gave a decisive advantage to Confederate forces.
   - **D.** It resulted in foreign recognition of the Confederacy.

4. What happened at Appomattox?
   - **A.** Lee stopped a Union advance.
   - **B.** Grant invaded Gettysburg.
   - **C.** Meade took control of Vicksburg.
   - **D.** Lee surrendered to Grant.

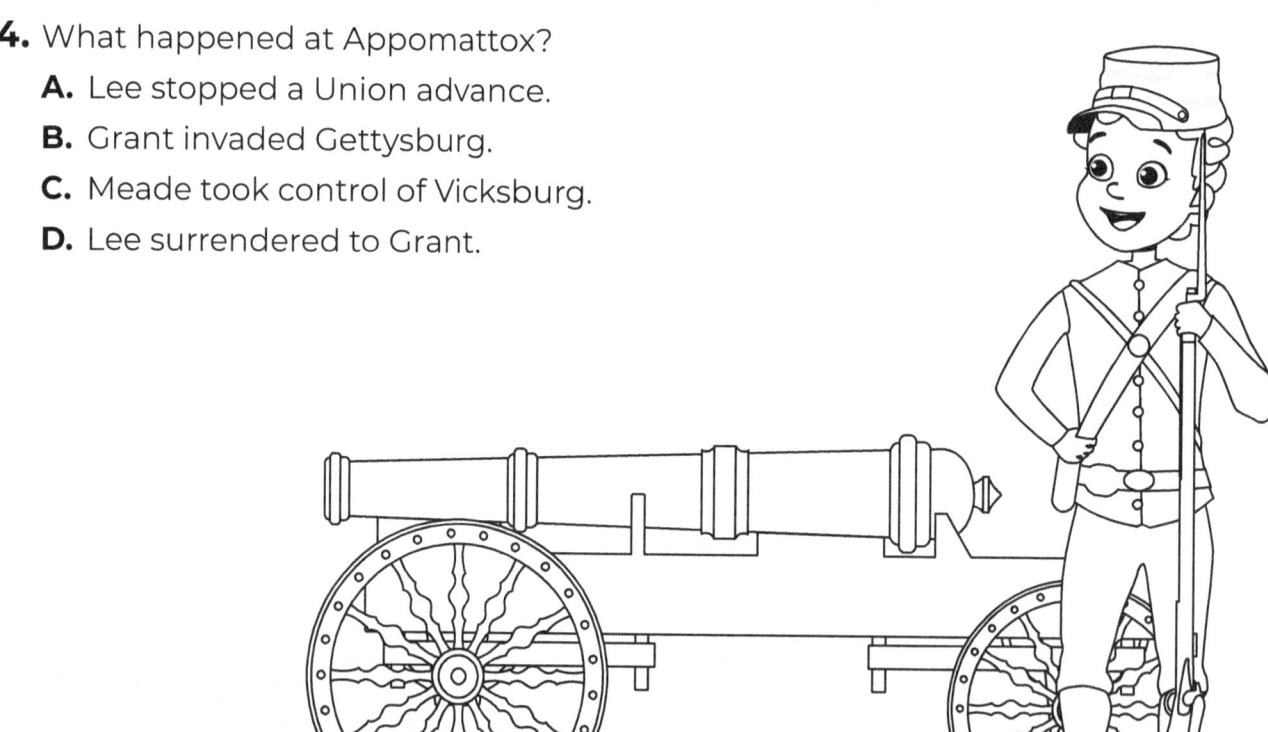

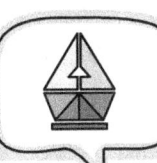
Directions: Read the text below. Then answer the questions that follow.

The Civil War has sometimes been called the first modern war because of its use of technology. The new technology was used with old, outdated battlefield tactics which led to a large amount of casualties. The chart below indicates some of the technological advances that made the Civil War so destructive.

		Impact
	Rifles	Rifles replaced muskets as the soldiers' main weapons. These weapons, with conical shaped ammunition, could shoot much farther and with more accuracy.
	Machine guns	The Gatling gun was the first gun that allowed armies to shoot multiple rounds in sustained fire. It was first used during the Civil War but was not widely adopted.

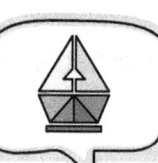
	Submarines	The H.L. *Hunley* was the first submarine in history to sink a warship. The boat destroyed the U.S.S. *Housatonic* in 1864. Submarines were not widely used during the war but did demonstrate their potential for undersea conflict.
	Ironclads	During the Civil War, both sides began to abandon the use of traditional wooden vessels for ships protected by steel plating called ironclads. This adoption changed the course of naval history and was first demonstrated in the battle between the *Monitor* and *Virginia* at Hampton Roads.
	Railroads	While railroads were not a new technology in the Civil War, they were an important one. Railroads were used to transport troops quickly to the conflict. This is where the Union had a clear advantage.
	Telegraph	The telegraph, which was developed in the 1830s and 1840s by Samuel Morse, was used to quickly relay information on the war to leaders in order to make quick decisions.

1. Which of the following was an advance in naval technology during the Civil War?

    A. Gatling guns

    B. ironclads

    C. rifles

    D. railroads

2. Which technology was not widely used during the Civil War?

    A. rifles

    B. ironclads

    C. submarines

    D. railroads

3. How was having more railroads an advantage for the Union?

    A. They were sources of additional monetary income.

    B. They could be converted to powerful weapons.

    C. They allowed for news to be communicated more quickly.

    D. They allowed for the quick transportation of troops.

4. What is one reason why the Civil War was so deadly?

    A. It used new technologies mixed with old tactics.

    B. It was the first war that saw genocide.

    C. It had few means of effectively communicating from the front.

    D. It used outdated equipment.

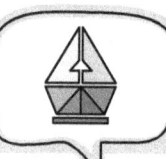
Directions: Read the text below. Then answer the questions that follow.

During the Civil War in 1864, Abraham Lincoln faced reelection. His success depended on the success of his generals. His opponent, Democratic candidate General **George B. McClellan**, promised to negotiate a peace between the Union and the Confederacy. However, the further successes of Union generals Ulysses S. Grant and William Tecumseh Sherman solidified Lincoln's reelection. Lincoln won a second term with 55 percent of the popular vote. Lincoln's win was in part because Union troops were allowed to vote from the battlefields. More than 155,000 soldiers voted this way and overwhelmingly voted for Lincoln. This was the first time **absentee voting** was used in American history. Lincoln viewed his victory as an opportunity to end slavery permanently. On January 31, 1865 after much debate, the **Thirteenth Amendment**, which ended slavery in the United States, passed through Congress and was sent to the states for ratification in December of that year. The Civil War effectively decided the issue of slavery. It also made it clear that no state could secede from the United States without drastic repercussions.

While the Civil War would end that May, Lincoln did not live to see it. On April 14, 1865, he was assassinated by the actor John Wilkes Booth at Ford's Theater in Washington, D.C. while seeing a play with his wife.

1. Who assassinated Abraham Lincoln?

  A. George B. McCellan

  B. William Tecumseh Sherman

  C. Jefferson Davis

  D. John Wilkes Booth

2. What innovation in democracy first appeared during the Civil War?

  A. secret ballots

  B. absentee voting

  C. women's suffrage

  D. voting booths

3. How did Lincoln view his reelection victory in 1864?

....

....

4. What issues did the Civil War decide?

....

....

Directions: Read the text below. Then answer the questions that follow.

The following passage is an excerpt from Abraham Lincoln's Second Inaugural Address, March 4, 1865:

"If we shall suppose that American slavery is one of those offenses which in the providence of God must needs come but which having continued through His appointed time He now wills to remove and that He gives to both North and South this terrible war as the woe due to those by whom the offense came shall we discern therein any departure from those divine attributes which the believers in a living God always ascribe to Him. Fondly do we hope, fervently do we pray that this mighty scourge of war may speedily pass away. Yet, if God wills that it continue until all the wealth piled by the bondsman's two hundred and fifty years of unrequited toil shall be sunk and until every drop of blood drawn with the lash shall be paid by another drawn with the sword as was said three thousand years ago so still it must be said 'the judgments of the Lord are true and righteous altogether.'

"With malice toward none with charity for all with firmness in the right as God gives us to see the right let us strive on to finish the work we are in to bind up the nation's wounds, to care for him who shall have borne the battle and for his widow and his orphan to do all which may achieve and cherish a just and lasting peace among ourselves and with all nations."

1. What position does Lincoln assume toward slavery in this address?

....

....

2. What is his position toward the South?

....

....

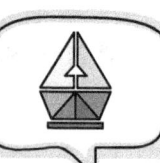

Directions: Read the text below. Then answer the questions that follow.

This week you learned about the conclusion of the Civil War and its impact on American history.

1. Was the end of the Civil War predictable based on your knowledge of the North and South? Explain why or why not.

2. How would fighting with rifles be different from fighting with muskets?

3. Do you think Lincoln's proposed *"With malice toward none with charity for all..."* was the appropriate course to take toward the South? What type of objections would be raised from it?

4. What issues of the Civil War have carried through to today?

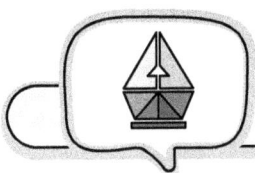

Answer Sheets

To see the answer key to the entire workbook, you can easily download the answer key from our website!

*Due to the high request from parents and teachers, we have removed the answer key from the workbook so you do not need to rip out the answer key while students work on the workbook.

To watch free video explanations go to: **argoprep.com/social7**
OR scan the QR Code:

Place your mouse over the workbook you have, and you will see the "Download Answers" button.

For detailed video instructions on how to access the "Answer Sheets," please scan this QR code.

Books explanations

All Books   Grade: All   Series: Social Studies   Search...

7th Grade Social Studies: Daily Practice Workbook

5th Grade Social Studies: Daily Practice Workbook

8th Grade Social Studies: Daily Practice Workbook

4th Grade Social Studies: Daily Practice Workbook

3rd Grade Social Studies: Daily Practice Workbook

8th Grade Social Studies: Daily

⬇ Download Answers

4th Grade Social Studies: Practice Workbook

www.ingramcontent.com/pod-product-compliance
Lightning Source LLC
Chambersburg PA
CBHW081326120626

46546CB00011B/3246